My Partner, BEN HOGAN

My Partner

BEN

HOGAN

by Jimmy Demaret

Drawings by Murray Olderman

McGraw-Hill Book Company, Inc.

New York   Toronto   London

HOUSTON PUBLIC LIBRARY

to JACK BURKE, SR.,
who made a professional golfer of me.
You can't repay a man for that

ACKNOWLEDGMENTS

Without the untiring efforts and editorial assistance of
JIMMY BRESLIN *and* HARRY GRAYSON
of NEA Service, Inc., this book would never have been written.

I also wish to acknowledge the valuable contributions of the following: John Brennan, of the Long Island Daily Press; *Harry Nash, of the* Newark Evening News; *Doug Ford; Al Ciuci; Fred Corcoran, of the P.G.A.; Joe Dey, of the U.S.G.A.; Dan Jenkins, of the* Fort Worth Telegram; *Hollis A. Goodrich; Toots Shor; Henry Picard; Ray Parker and Arthur Winarick, of the Concord Hotel; Guido Cribari, of the Westchester County, N.Y., Newspapers; John Derr, of the Columbia Broadcasting System; and Bob Brumby.*

CONTENTS

LIST OF ILLUSTRATIONS

CHAPTER 1

BEN AND ME

For years now, I've been sitting in my living room in Houston, Texas, or in my pro shop at the Concord International Hotel in the Catskills, reading books about golf. Just about every one of them has been authored by one of my fellow playing pros. In fact, so many of my golfing pals have been punching a typewriter between tournament dates that an awful lot of people were beginning to stare at me, wondering what was wrong.

"Do you think he's illiterate?" I heard one fellow whisper behind my back this fall. Well, I guess this immortal publication should end that kind of talk.

But no matter how many of the boys are batting out books these days, it still seems like a strange development to me. When an author decides to take up golf, it causes little concern in the literary world. It usually means that he or she intends to relax. But when a golfer takes up writing—unless he's collaborating with, say, Kathleen Winsor on a historical golfing novel—it always lifts my eyebrows. And they rose exceptionally high—in fact they disappeared right into

1

my receding hairline—when recently I began a book written by a famous golfer and close friend of mine. One of the first instructional pages started out something like this: "When you bring the clubhead back, avoid the convolutional pivot but flex both the deltoid and bicep to prevent pre-stroke rigidity."

Now I've known the author for over fifteen years and never heard him say anything heavier than "It's your shot." He is one of those golfers who just swings away and plays a great game, but I'm dead certain he has absolutely no idea what makes him play so well. He's a natural. He was born with that swing.

When these golfer-authors sit down to put a book together, it is usually for the purpose of telling the reader how to take shots off his score by using a better grip, a different swing, a superior stance, and a few thousand other tricks of the trade. But I like to believe that this book is something different. My hope is that it will help contribute in some small way to what we now know as the Ben Hogan Legend. History is going to show that the tremendous victories put together by this little fellow from Texas have meant more to the game of golf than any event in years.

This book is the story of golf as I've seen it, and the story of Ben Hogan as I know it. It is about a hard-bitten little caddy from Dublin, Texas, who has become the finest golf player of the mid-twentieth century. What Hogan's career stands for, nationally and internationally, is of vital interest to myself, the rest of my golfing colleagues, and the whole sports-loving world. Ben has given golf a great modern hero. The graceful manner in which he has accepted what fancy sports writers call the mantle of greatness has meant more in good will toward golf than any single act on or off a course for the past twenty years. They always say that Francis Ouimet took golf off the sports pages and put it on the front page. Well, Hogan went even further than Ouimet, America's first big international golf name. Little Ben actually put golf on the editorial page with his victory in the British Open at Carnoustie, Scotland, in 1953. Political issues were pushed aside and even *The New York Times'* solemn editorial page cracked a smile of welcome on the occasion of Hogan's triumphant return to this country.

What happened to Adlai Stevenson on his tour of Europe last year bears me out. When the Democratic leader was in England, he said he thought that he would have won our last Presidential election if Europeans had been allowed to vote. Later, a member of the House of Lords, when told of Stevenson's remark, commented that Adlai was only the second most popular American, as far as England was concerned.

"Who is the top man?" a concerned Stevenson aide asked. "President Eisenhower?"

"No," the English bigwig replied. "Ben Hogan."

Now I'm not trying to get myself involved in a political fight. My game is golf. In fact, that column on Ben had me turning to the editorial page for the first time in twenty-five years. But I do know that there is a lot of truth about the Hogan part of that story. Ben, right now, rates one-two with the most popular figures in sports history. They love him in Dublin, Texas, where he was born, but they love him in England and on the Continent, too.

If there is anybody in golf who knows Ben Hogan and understands what makes him tick, it's Jimmy Demaret. Together we formed one of the best four-ball teams golf has ever known (he says modestly). Out of the miles we've walked together on the links, a very close friendship has developed.

I've known Ben since 1932 and pride myself on being one of the few people in golf he'll listen to. That may sound like loud talk, but it's plain and simple fact. I even had a little to do with talking Ben into going to Scotland for the British Open when he came up to my Concord Hotel course for an exhibition. There had been rumors going the rounds of his trying for the British crown—this was just before he took his fourth United States Open in six years—but Ben said he didn't want to make the trip.

"What would I want to go over there for?" He shrugged. "What would it prove? I don't like boats. I don't like flying. They tell me the food is bad and a decent hotel room is next to impossible to get. Besides, what do I have to gain?"

"You owe it to the game," I told him, and I meant it sincerely. Everybody in golf could see what a Hogan victory in the British Open would mean. Everybody, that is, but Ben. He didn't think he was that important. So I worked on him a little bit. "You're a legend over there, Ben. They want to see you. Carnoustie is where golf came from. It's supposed to be a great course."

It would mean a great deal to the Scots. For years they had been hearing of this marvelous golfer America had developed, and they wanted to see him. The British press, in particular, was marking time. They had witnessed Bobby

Jones's failure on his first try and they'd seen Walter Hagen "pick up" during his opening round. They wanted to see what Hogan would do. If he lost, they would be able to say, once again, "You Americans have fine golfers . . . but not over here!"

So I worked on Ben a little more. "I don't see you going over," he objected.

"Why, Ben, a fella like me has to work for a living," I answered. "We all can't have that sockful you carry around." I was referring to what people with large vocabularies might call Ben's "affluence." The last thing in the world Ben Hogan has to worry about is money. We argued back and forth for another few minutes and then he left the shop. The next day he drove down from the Lake Kiamesha course, dropped into Golf House in New York City, and casually entered the British Open. Later in the summer he went to Scotland and made history. I like to feel that I had a little something to do with helping make the Hogan Legend.

To my mind, Ben Hogan is the greatest golfer that ever lived, and I don't have to go far to get a lot of people to back me up. I've played with and against him, as boy and veteran, for twenty-two years. When we hooked up as the team of Hogan and Demaret nobody touched us in four-ball competition. We won four Miami Internationals and as many Inverness Round Robin Four-Ball events. We were undefeated playing on Ryder Cup teams in Portland, Oregon, in 1947, and in Pinehurst, North Carolina, in 1951. We played together on Bobby Jones's and Gene Sarazen's American challenge team against Ryder Cup aggregations at Detroit in 1940 and 1941 and won both times.

As partners, Ben, the quiet and intense one, kept toning down Demaret, who, it must be admitted, inclines toward wildness and gaiety at inappropriate moments. We two almost opposite personalities helped each other a good deal. I kept everybody around me loose and Ben's strict concentration was enough to keep me on the ball.

It was out of our four-ball partnership that I first gained real respect for Hogan as a golfer. He had played in the first tournament I ever won, the Texas P.G.A. in Dallas in 1934, and he came in about twentieth. Ben had begun tournament golf three years before, in 1932, but it wasn't until 1940 that he won a tournament of any note. With a lot of failures sapping his spirit and emptying his purse, Ben had to wait all those years before he began to earn the big money with major victories. Only a four-ball victory with Vic Ghezzi in the Hershey Invitational in 1938 broke the disheartening spell of defeats. His record was spotty during those lean years. He took only a twelfth in the Hershey Open in 1937; a second in the Phoenix Open in 1939, a tie for third in that year's Oakland Open. "It looks like I'm never going to win a tournament," Ben would say mournfully. But while he was saying it, Jimmy Demaret, unerring prophet, was telling everyone within earshot that "this is the best golfer in the country right now." Like no one else, I knew Hogan's game and character intimately, and I was certain that such a combination couldn't be held down for long. History has proved me right. In 1940, Ben won a flock of major tournaments, the North and South at Pinehurst, the Hershey Open, and many others. He wound up as the leading money winner with $10,656. Everyone who ever turns to the sports page knows that he has been right up there ever since.

As for one James Demaret, he always likes to recall, if no one else is going to mention it, that he is the only three-time winner of the Masters Tournament. He also would like to have it whispered around that he can't let his partner, Ben Hogan, steal too much of a stride on him. That's correct. Demaret is going over to win the British Open this year.

Down in Houston, where I live most of the year, they'll tell you my official title is "Houston's Ambassador to the World." Texas feels it needs more than just congressmen to tell its story. We have always felt that informal ambassadors to foreign countries were important, and since I travel so much, and Texas certainly rates an ambassador, they gave me the title. The boys around the golf circuit call me several things; the "Man of Many Hats" is one of the few that I can repeat in print. You might say they are accurate on that one. I own 43 lids at the moment, ranging from a scotch-plaid fedora to the wildest tam you ever did see. I prefer extra-bright colors on the rest of the things around me too, starting with my red-haired wife, Idella. In the clothes department, I have 71 pairs of slacks, 20 jerseys, 55 shirts, and 39 sports coats. I'm partial to brick red, mulberry, royal crimson, pale pink, purple, hunter green, nile green, heather green, and flaming scarlet. I learned early that color puts life into things.

My clothes are important, but I also have what some people call an adequate golf game. Aside from my Masters and four-ball victories, I've won such as the Los Angeles Open, St. Paul Open, and Miami Open, and in 1947 came through with enough victories to make me the leading professional money winner for that year with $27,936. However, 1940, when I won six of nine tournaments, including the Masters, was my big year. I was even able to hang onto enough money so that I needed only a small loan for carfare home. My average for 34 competitive rounds in all kinds of weather was a 70.7. In the Masters I went completely wild on the back nine and shot the Augusta course in 30, a somewhat unbelievable record which left nobody more amazed than Demaret. It makes me feel so good just to talk about it that I yearn to describe it to you stroke by stroke. If there ever was one round a golfer could point to and say, "That made me for life," I can point to that back nine at Augusta. I had twelve putts for the nine holes and came away with six birdies and three pars. Whenever things get tough nowadays in my middle age, I pick up my scrapbook and read about that round. I still think the newspapermen who covered it should have received Pulitzer prizes for their stories. Best reading I've ever done.

In my memory file, the Masters win just noses out my first major tournament victory for excitement. That was the San Francisco Match Play Championship in 1938, when I defeated the veteran White Sulphur Springs author and comedian, Samuel Jackson Snead. My first tournament victory came a long time before that, however. In 1923, when I was all of twelve, I toured the Hermann Park course at Houston in 83 to win the city caddy championship. Two years later, I repeated with a 74, when I was fourteen. I'd settle for that fourteen-year-old form today.

But more important than these victories is the thirty-year love affair I've had with the game of golf itself. I like to win, maybe a bit more than the next fellow, but I also like golf, the greatest game that anyone ever dreamed up. The old phrase, "It's an 'umbling game," seems truer than ever today. You don't need a partner or an opponent. You just walk out there with yourself, your God, and your eight iron for a lesson in humility. That's something folks need a lot more of these days.

In addition, golf has given me friends I wouldn't trade for all the oil in Texas. My fellow pros are the finest men alive, and traveling the golf circuit year after year I've seen a lot of them. The other nice folks I've met on the fairways of the world, from kings and presidents right down to Mr. Average Duffer, they're all the same. The game of golf attracts fine people. I have made friendships on golf courses around the world which mean more to me than a hatful of victories or pockets full of money. The little things in golf count, too: the crack from a brassie which means you've caught one just right; those anxious moments in the locker room when you finish a tournament and wonder if your 280 is going to hold up; a fine flash of humor from a wisecracking caddy that does so much to relieve the tension.

Locker rooms during a tournament bring to mind the United States Open in 1948, played at the Riviera Country Club near Los Angeles. Now, the Open isn't the richest tournament in the country, but it's the most important. It carries the most prestige. I finished the four rounds with a

278, a record score for the Open, if only for a few hours, and one which still stands today as the second best ever made. It is three strokes better than any other golfer has been able to shoot—except for ᵗhe fellow who was still out on the course that June day in 1948. He was, of course, Ben Hogan. The little man, under tremendous pressure, was clipping the ball pretty well that afternoon, even for him. Three hours later, his 276 was posted ahead of my "record." Sitting in the locker room watching minutes tick by, I'd lost the U.S. Open to my best friend.

When I hear a lot of misinformed people talk about Hogan's disregard for others and his cold ruthlessness, I always think of that day. After he had won, Ben walked up to me and said serious-like (he still knows no other way), "Jimmy, I'm glad I won, but I'm sorry I had to beat you." That's the kind of talk and sentiment I've always heard from Ben. He meant every word of it.

Hogan and I are close friends, but when we walk onto the course for a competitive round against each other nothing counts except the score. Consider, for instance, the semifinals of the Professional Golfers' Association Championship at the Portland, Oregon, Golf Club in 1946. My pal Ben beat me by a little matter of 10 and 9. He was concentrating that day.

"What was the turning point, Jimmy?" a writer asked me afterward.

"When we teed off at ten o'clock," I told him.

I guess you could compare Ben and me, when we're competing against each other, to the two Scotsmen who were playing at the hallowed St. Andrews. There was a shilling or two involved in the match and a certain amount of tension was felt on the scene. One of the players boomed his shot toward the green on the eighteenth hole, but it wasn't visible whether he had made it or not. His opponent turned to his caddy and said, "Is my wurra good friend in the trap or is the sonofabitch on the green?"

Despite all the pressure of tournament competition, I have always remembered something a fine man told me when I was a green kid in Houston. "Jimmy," he said, "there is a lot more to golf than just hitting a ball—sportsmanship, friends, a whole way of life. You'll find as you go along that you receive as much from the game as you give it. Don't forget that." The man was Jack Burke, Sr., in whose Houston golf shop I used to work. I've done my level best not to forget what he told me.

The game of golf has meant everything in my life. Without it, I would have spent my days trying to make a living in a factory or a shop. Instead, most of my working hours have been spent on beautiful golf courses all over the world. Not only have I had the pleasure of meeting people in all walks of life, but golf has given me an education, too. I never did have the opportunity of entering those ivy-covered collegiate halls when I was a youngster. In fact, the second year of Houston's North Side High School was the zenith of my classroom career. Though even today I don't enjoy competing against Rhodes scholars on quiz programs, nevertheless golf has given me an education of sorts. I've been in many parts of the world. I know America as well as any man alive. Every year I put in about 60,000 miles of traveling, which has given me a solid education in everything from economics (gas is cheaper in New Jersey) to psychology (if you keep talking to an opponent who has a tough shot coming up, he may blow it).

As a member of the 1949 Ryder Cup team, I went to England on the *Queen Elizabeth* and gave London and its historical sites (also its brighter spots) a thorough once over. I make a yearly trip to Havana and twice paid visits to South America's version of Texas—Argentina. In fact, most of Latin America, from the pampas to Mexico, has been under my scrutiny at one time or another. I've played golf in Brazil, Chile, Guatemala, Nicaragua, El Salvador, Panama, Venezuela, and Uruguay. In 1952, Lloyd Mangrum, Jim Turnesa, Ed Oliver, and I flew to Australia to revive the old Lakes Cup Matches and we toured the land down under from Adelaide to Sydney, playing the best courses it has to offer. Australia, incidentally, gave me the biggest surprise of my foreign golf travels. When we began our tour down there, I found tennis, generally considered the country's national game, running a poor third to horse racing and golf. Australia is a golfer's paradise; the world doesn't boast a finer spot for a swinger than Melbourne, a city which sits in what is known as the great sand belt. On it are located some of the world's finest golf courses. Just outside of town they have a veritable "golf city" with ten courses bordering on one another, each one rating with the finest in the world. Any of our American "golf widows" who think things are rough in New York or Los Angeles or Chicago can thank their lucky stars they don't live in Melbourne. They'd just never see their husbands.

A golf course is a great equalizer. When you walk out on

300 acres of rolling green and begin playing and watching your mistakes, it brings you down to earth, whether your name is Eisenhower, Demaret, or Schultz. More important, perhaps, is the fact that golf is built on honesty. There are no referees in the normal golf match and ugly squabbles are usually nonexistent. A fellow marks down "4" on his scorecard when he shoots a 4 and if he takes a 10, then that "10" goes down. You can't help but like a person who'll come up to you and say, usually in language that turns the air blue, "I had a bad hole, took a seven that time," when you haven't been keeping track of his shots. Perhaps this basic honesty which prevails in golf is partially responsible for attracting such fine people to the sport.

Take the example of Lloyd Mangrum in the United States Open in 1950, for instance. At a crucial point in an eighteen-hole playoff with Ben Hogan and George Fazio for the title, Lloyd bent down and lifted his ball to remove a bug from its surface. Because the crawling thing was disturbing his concentration, he simply picked up the ball, blew the bug off, and then put it down in the same spot. Immediately a two-stroke penalty was called under the U.S.G.A. rules. Under the P.G.A. rules, picking up the ball for such a purpose is allowed, but the U.S. Open is played under United States Golf Association rules. When informed of the penalty, Mangrum quietly asked that the rule be read to him. Then he asked that it be read a second time. Finally he shrugged and said, "Fair enough. We'll all eat tomorrow, no matter what happens." Without even the suggestion of a complaint, he took the two-stroke penalty and eventually lost the play-off to Hogan. And the United States Open, my friends, when you consider the endorsements and other commercial opportunities which come in its wake, is worth a cool $100,000 or more to the winner.

I've met more interesting folks in my way of life than Grover Whelan has in his. A round with the Duke of Windsor or ex-King Carol of Rumania or ex-King Leopold of Belgium is just as exciting as eighteen holes with Vice-president Nixon. For that matter, a fast tour of a course in Toledo, Ohio, with two or three friends named Joe is the best way to spend an afternoon that I know of. People—all people —seem to exhibit their best selves on a golf course.

And now I'd like to attempt to pay off at least a small part of that enormous debt I owe the world of golf by putting down on paper all that I know about the game and its greatest asset, my partner Ben Hogan.

CHAPTER 2

THIS GAME OF GOLF

When Teddy Roosevelt brought his hunting equipment to Washington, D.C., at the turn of the century, grandpa didn't rush for his shotgun and blast away at everything this side of the bear rug. And when Harry Truman came all the way from Missouri with his baby grand and the "Missouri Waltz," the boys still were passing up piano recitals in favor of that regular Saturday afternoon poker game. But when popular demand established Dwight D. Eisenhower as the playing pro on the tough White House course, the nation began a frantic rush to golf courses and driving ranges. Three and a half million par-hungry American duffers hailed Ike as the best thing to happen in golf since Mac-Gregor put out the Jimmy Demaret clubs and Chester Hogan introduced his son Ben to golf.

The impact that the team of Eisenhower and Hogan has had on golf the world over is as powerful as the blast from a country boy's shotgun. Hogan's victories put world golf interest at an all-time peak. From Melbourne to Chicago, people talked and read about his British triumph. Then when the President of the United States posed with one of those "Don't Ask Me What I Shot" buttons, golf enthusiasts went crazy.

In fact, golf has reached the point where a little cottage on the grounds of the Augusta National course has been dubbed "The Summer White House" by reporters who follow Eisenhower around. The President spends vacations at that cottage, dividing his time between work important to the nation and trying to lick that tough par-five sixteenth hole. Most of the newspaper pictures during this period dealt with Ike and his battle against par. Later in the summer of 1953, however, I noted a heavy influx of photos showing the President trying his hand at trout fishing in Colorado. The fishing lobby must have gotten to him.

Then late in 1953, Adlai Stevenson, the Democratic Presidential candidate in 1952, further strengthened the bond between golf and national politics. In a speech in Atlanta, Stevenson, in looking forward to the next Presidential election, slipped easily into golfing lingo. "I'm not interested in shooting under 90," he said. "I'd rather shoot 108 —out in 52 and back in 56." It looks as if everybody wants to get in on the act.

Now golf is an old game, one that goes back more than 500 years, but I don't think it ever has received the lift Hogan's victory in Scotland and Ike's chase after par gave it in 1953. The heights the game has reached today are a good long holler from the way golfers were treated back in 1457, when the Scottish Parliament passed a law prohibiting the playing of golf so that young men would put more time in on archery for national defense. And thirty years from now, when Ben Hogan and I are down in Texas rocking on the front porch and fondling our Social Security checks, I think the game will have attained an eminence of which we can only dream today.

Golf, in my opinion, is still in its infancy. By its very nature, it demands more time to develop than baseball, football, or other popular games. Kids can always find an empty lot for a baseball game, but it takes a lot of money in your jeans to build an eighteen-hole golf course. But, with this twin-barreled push the White House and Hogan have given the game, in the near future American mass-production methods, brought into action by mass demand, will bring the financial aspect of golf right down to meet a newsboy's pocket.

Right here, it might be well to try to answer the question that a man in a sand trap always asks himself. I'm talking about the fellow who is two good iron shots from the green but right now lies six in a trap which looks like a bomb crater. "Where did this game come from?" the fellow asks. "And more important, who's the guy who invented it? I'd sure like to meet up with *him*."

That reminds me of a story—I know you won't mind a short detour—of the too-eager social worker who came to my home in Houston several years ago. She was calling on my laundress, a fine Negro lady with eight children. The social worker was well loaded down with notebooks and busting apart with knowledge. You know, the kind of young, just-out-of-college gal who's itching to be asked about her education so she can start shoving sheepskins at you. Well, she became right curious about one of the children, a little boy whose bright red hair and blue eyes just weren't in keeping with the color scheme of the seven other kids.

The questions flew thick and fast and my laundress just sat there and kept nodding. Finally, she had enough. "Look, honey," she told the interviewer. "Let's not worry so much where he come from. Let's just rejoice that he's here."

And that's the way I've always felt about golf.

Historians have argued the point for a long time. Just about every kid in America can tell you that Abner Doubleday invented baseball at Cooperstown, New York, in 1839, and that a fellow by the name of Dr. James Naismith set up a game called basketball at Springfield, Massachusetts, in 1891. But even the top golfers say, hazily, "the game started over in Scotland." That's about all most of them can tell you.

As a starter, you can make a little money betting against Scotland as the birthplace of golf. The first course was located in England, at a place called Blackheath, a high-lying common—that's an open space, I'm told—about 5 miles southeast of London in the county of Kent. It was opened at the time of James I (who also was James IV of Scotland, everybody knows that) in 1603, and later the course became known as the Royal Blackheath Golf Club.

We golf historians call this the Feather Ball Period, and it was to last until 1848. The feather ball was the first golf ball. It consisted of a cowhide cover around a core of wetted feathers. The stems were removed and the feathers pounded to a pulp. Douglas Gourlay and his family at Musselburgh, Scotland, were the foremost feather-ball makers. Their home town was aptly named. It took a lot of muscle to move that feather ball, not only because it died in flight but also because it wasn't completely rounded. I've seen one of those early feather balls, and the man who could putt with one just hasn't been born.

The very earliest clubs were crude, but near the end of the Feather Ball Period they were making them long, thin, and graceful. The shafts were whippy and the grips thick. Hugh Philip and Douglas McEwan were the foremost clubmakers of that day, the Chippendale and Hepplewhite of clubmaking, so to speak. The full, free style which has become known as the "St. Andrews Swing" developed out of this early period, and the graceful clubs were partly responsible. The Neanderthal Man of clubmaking was one William Mayne of Edinburgh, who received a royal warrant from James VI as clubmaker and spearmaker in 1603. There is an old notebook from this period which indicates that Mayne received payments for repairs on "play clubis," "Bonker clubis" and an "irone club." There are no examples of Mayne's clubs in existence today, but some of them are pictured in art from that period and they are crude. The oldest set of clubs in existence is a group of six woods and two irons, which are kept at the Troon Golf Club in Scotland. It is whispered about that they date back to 1741, and all are ash-shafted. Only one wood and one iron have grips. The pro's stamp is too worn for identification, but the golf historians say they could have been made by Andrew Dickson, of Leith, or Henry Mill, of St. Andrews, well-known clubmakers of the era.

Despite this evidence, the intensive Demaret research produced another theory for a time: namely, that the game might have originated in Holland and been later introduced to

Scotland by sea captains who had seen a similar sport, called "kolven," played on the ice in Holland. One piece of evidence is an old Dutch tapestry I've seen. It shows two men standing with slim sticks, each stick having a knob on one end. The two men seem to be talking intensely about something, as though one burgher is arguing that he actually lies four. What almost sold me on the authenticity of the Dutch claim was that his partner is quietly nudging what is obviously a golf ball out of a gopher hole with one of his wooden shoes. Perhaps history shows that this wasn't the first real golf game, but it certainly is the first application of winter rules on record. Modern "kolven," however, little resembles golf. It doesn't seem too likely, despite our two burghers, that the game began in Holland.

By 1750, the British had three courses over which to stroll and lose their tempers. All were north of the Tweed River, the dividing line between England and Scotland. These three were the Edinburgh Burghers Golf Society, started in 1735, the Honourable Edinburgh Company of golfers in 1744, and in 1754 the organization we now know as the Royal and Ancient—St. Andrews—was founded. It was at St. Andrews that the first set of golf rules were drawn up, thirteen in number, and nine are still in our present-day rule book. The original thirteen are:

1. You must tee your ball within club length of the hole. (Today tees and greens are separated.)
2. Your tee must be above ground. (This is important for all United Mine Workers but I don't see how it applies to the rest of us.)

3. You are not to change ball which you strike off the tee. (We still retain this one.)

4. You are not to remove stones, bones, or any break-club for the sake of playing ball except on fairgreen and only within club length. (We still abide by this one, although I haven't been bothered by many bones lately. They must have had some rugged courses in those days.)

5. If ball come among water or any watery filth, you are at liberty to take the ball out and throw it 6 yards behind you and you may play it with any club and take a stroke for so getting out your ball. (We have kept this one, too.)

6. If your ball be found anywhere touching, lift the first ball, then play your own and replace the first ball. (We keep this one.)

7. At holing, you are to play your ball honestly for hole, but not to play upon your opponent's ball not lying in your way to hole. (Though a bit difficult to figure out, this is what makes play on the green different from a wicked game of croquet.)

8. If you should lose your ball, you are to go back to the spot where you played it from, drop another, and take a stroke for the misfortune. (We've kept this one.)

9. No man, at holing his ball, is allowed to mark the green with a channel or ditch. (I've come up with some wild ideas about how to drop a putt, but this tops them all.)

10. If a ball hits a person, horse, dog, or anything else, the ball is to be played where it lies. (That goes today, and, as we'll show later, is sometimes a major factor in tournament golf.)

11. If you draw the club in order to strike the ball and

twist it so far as to bring down club and if then it will break, you are to suffer a stroke. (Does that mean the guy drops dead? Or just loses a stroke?)

12. He whose ball is away, plays the first shot. (Still true.)

13. Neither trench, ditch, or dike made for the preservation of the course or scholar's holes, or soldier's lines shall be hazards, but ball is to be taken out and teed up and played with any iron. (Let's hope we don't have any Maginot Lines on our golf courses. As for the scholar's holes, I just don't know.)

After the Feather Ball Period, golf moved into the Gutta Percha Ball Period, which began in 1848 and ended in 1901. It was during this time that the game reached North America. From England and Scotland, golf was exported to other continents during the early part of the nineteenth century, usually by British Army officers. They had a club at Calcutta in 1829, another at Bombay in 1842, and were said to have played the game on the European continent as early as 1814.

The gutta-percha ball itself helped the game to spread. The first ball of this improved type was produced by the Reverend Dr. Robert Adams Patterson in 1845 from the gutta-percha packing used in shipping statues from India. The balls were made under "Patterson's patent," were brown in color and were made by rolling the gutta percha on a flat board. It had longer life, cost less than the feather ball, gave improved flight and truer run on the greens, and didn't fall apart in the rain. Thus even the clergy made its contribution to golf.

The clubs changed with the advent of the new ball, too. The slender clubs of the previous era had to be discarded as the new and harder ball demanded tougher sticks. The wooden heads became shorter and squatter in shape and leather inserts appeared on the faces. Irons increased in variety, and by the early 1890s the first bags were brought into use to carry the increased number of clubs. With better balls to hit and more people inventing new shots, the clubmakers developed a variety of sticks. Instead of five or six, the serious golfer in those days had thirteen clubs to choose from. They included seven woods (driver, bulger driver, long spoon, brassie, middle spoon, short spoon, putter) and six irons (cleek, midiron, lofting iron, mashie, niblick, and cleek putter).

It was during this period that the first golf club was established on our continent—the Royal Montreal in 1873. The Quebec club was established in 1875 and the Toronto club a year later. These three are the granddaddy courses of the North American continent and are all still in operation today.

However, the New World's first putt was holed in New York City almost a century before. During the Revolutionary War, British officers and Tories used to play a game closely resembling today's golf, but exactly where they played is not known. Old newspaper clippings also refer to the game being played at Charleston, South Carolina, as early as 1786 and at Savannah, Georgia, in 1795.

Probably because the game was essentially British, it was all but forgotten by Americans in the nineteenth century until it was reintroduced in 1884 at the Oakhurst Club, White Sulphur Springs, West Virginia. The club, however, had only a brief existence, because of financial troubles. The present-day course at White Sulphur Springs, at the famous Greenbrier Hotel, has for its pro the eminent Mr. Sam Snead, West Virginia's great gift to golf.

On February 22, 1888, John G. Reid, who is considered by many to be "The Father of American Golf," opened a three-hole course in an old apple orchard in Yonkers on the Hudson River just outside of New York. Reid, who was a transplanted Scot, named his three-holer St. Andrews after the original Scottish course. This executive of the Mott Haven Iron Works and a friend, Robert Lockhart, played their first round with three woods, three irons, and two dozen gutta-percha balls purchased in Scotland from the St. Andrews pro, Tom Morris.

Other clubs followed and in March of 1891 an important golf personage arrived in this country. His name was Willie Dunn and he was a Scottish pro. He settled in Southampton on Long Island and took over the pro shop at the Shinnecock Hills Club, where he began making those fine hickory-shafted clubs for Long Island players. He met with fine success, and a number of his fellow pros from Scotland soon were arriving on these shores to compete for the American market. The Chicago Club at Wheaton, Illinois, and the Country Club at Brookline, Massachusetts, were also established in the 1890s, and both of them are impressive tests of golf even today.

The year 1901 marked another major change in golf with the introduction of the rubber ball, which we still use today. Coburn Haskell, a Cleveland golfer, and Bertram G. Work of the Goodrich Rubber Company invented a ball which had a black hand-lined gutta-percha cover with tension-wound rubber thread on a solid rubber core inside. Dave Foulis, a Chicago professional, put one of the balls in an Agrippa mold and produced the bramble marking which was common in that day. Arguments flew back and forth about the ball being too lively to control—it far outdrove a gutta-percha ball—but they were settled when Walter J. Travis used a Haskell ball from the Agrippa mold in winning the U.S.G.A. Amateur Championship in 1901. Haskell balls at this time were light and large, about 1.55 ounces in weight and 1.71 inches in diameter. It was not until 1932 that a standard ball of 1.62 ounces and 1.68 inches was introduced by the U.S.G.A. When in 1942 it was ruled that a ball must not be "hopped up" to travel more than 250 feet per second, the specifications for the modern golf ball were finally and completely set.

Close to every pro's heart are new clubs, whether he's selling them or playing with them. The Industrial Revolution caught up with the game at the beginning of the twentieth century and the old craftsman who spent long hours making clubs in his pro shop soon was displaced by modern machines which stamped them out like cookies. Important changes were made in club styles, with persimmon and laminated clubheads appearing with the faces machine-lined to increase the spin on the ball in flight. Next, stainless-steel shafts replaced hickory. In fact so many other innovations were being introduced that the Royal and Ancient Golf Club wisely announced, in 1908, that it would not sanction any substantial departure from the traditional form and make of golf clubs. This rule still goes today and is an excellent controlling factor. In 1938 the U.S.G.A. limited the number of clubs a player could use in one round to fourteen. With this regulation, the traditional names for each club soon were dropped by manufacturers and replaced by the numbers we use today.

Equipment kept pace with the times and, happily for American golf, so did the players. The golfers who could get people truly excited about the sport began to appear on the American links. About 1903, Willie Anderson proved himself a fine player, but the first American-born golfer to win the U.S. Open was a cocky little Philadelphian named Johnny McDermott. Johnny confidently predicted that he would be the first home-bred golfer to defeat the superior players trained in England and Scotland, and he astonished the country by making good on his prediction. He won the U.S. Open two years in succession, at the Chicago Golf Club in 1911 and at the Country Club of Buffalo in 1912, and probably would have gone on to greater successes had not a tragic mental illness cut short his golfing career. McDermott, incidentally, grew up in Philadelphia with Jack Burke, Sr., the fine gent who taught me so much about the game of golf.

Looking back, I'd say that it wasn't until 1913 that the first "big man" arrived on the scene. He was Francis Ouimet. Now I don't intend to rate the best golfers of all time here. I haven't either the knowledge or the nerve. I'm just going straight to the record for the ones who made the heaviest impression on the public and gave golf its biggest boost when it most needed it.

But it's a matter of record that Francis made the big splash. It was Ouimet—you pronounce it "Wee-met"—who reached out and touched Mr. Average American for the first time in golf history. Until this ex-caddy, unknown except around Boston, walked onto the course and amazed the world by winning the United States Open in 1913, the game of golf was essentially a pastime for the president of the United States Steel and his wealthy friends. It was a good deal too expensive for the average fellow, and with traditional American disdain for anything highbrow, golf was ignored and even ridiculed by the person who makes this country tick— the man in the street.

Ouimet did a lot toward changing all this with one tournament—a tournament which was played right across the street from his modest home at Brookline, Massachusetts. Francis came from nowhere in 1913 to beat Harry Vardon and Ted Ray, two fine British golfers, in a playoff for the U.S. Open crown. After people got through asking each other who Ouimet was, golf was on its way toward popularity in this country. Ouimet, they found out, was just a normal youth who hailed from an average working-class family which lived in a middle-income-bracket house in Brookline. The only thing special about the house was its proximity to the venerable Brookline Country Club. Francis hiked across its fairways on his way to school and eventually drifted into the business every kid who lives near a golf course must engage in—finding lost balls and converting them into cash or something else useful. The "something useful" in this instance was a set of clubs which Francis and his brother earned over a period of months by trading three dozen balls for a club with a Boston sporting-goods house. The "set of clubs," it should be pointed out, consisted of three, two coming from the sporting-goods house and the third from the Country Club course.

Francis was too young to go across the street and caddy, as his older brother was doing, so he stayed in his back yard and practiced on a homemade course consisting of a swamp, a gravel pit, and tin cans for holes. As soon as he was eleven, he joined the bag-toting ranks and began to practice on the Country Club course itself. At fifteen he formed the Brookline High golf team and won the Greater Boston Schoolboy title. Golf now became the big thing in Ouimet's life. When the U.S. Amateur was scheduled to be played across the street at the Country Club in 1910, he borrowed $25 from his mother to join the nearby Woodland Golf Club. (To be eligible for the Amateur in those days, it was necessary to be a member of a recognized club.) But the $25 didn't come easily—and this humble beginning was one of the factors which captured the imagination of the American public. Francis went to work in a Boston store for $4 a week to pay off the debt to his mother. He didn't qualify for the Amateur that year, missing out by one stroke. The same thing happened in 1911 and 1912. The next year, one of the biggest in early American golf history, Ouimet not only qualified but went to the semifinals in the National Amateur before bowing.

The Open was next on the list for the Country Club and

it never entered Ouimet's mind to enter it. When friends approached him about it, he turned down all talk of entering on the theory that he just was not ready for it. But Robert Watson, the president of the U.S.G.A., thought the contrary and finally won out in a talk with Ouimet. The two British stars, Vardon and Ray, were considered sure things to place one-two in the Open. They had been on tour in this country and had created a big impression with their exhibitions. When Vardon led the first-day qualifiers with 151, a stroke ahead of the twenty-year-old Ouimet, it caused little excitement. Ray came back with a 148 on the second day and when the actual tourney medal play began, people were even more certain that victory would eventually go to one of the two British stars.

But at the end of fifty-four holes, something was stirring. Vardon and Ray were tied for the lead all right, each with 225. But the kid from across the street, Francis Ouimet, carded the same score. And, when Ray and Vardon finished the next eighteen holes in a tie at 304 and Ouimet finished in with two birdies to stay right with them, the excitement reached nationwide proportions. There was to be an eighteen-hole playoff among the three. Now the first faint rustling of interest in American fans grew into an ardent hope. Perhaps young Ouimet wasn't a fluke. Maybe he had a chance. The first nine holes of the playoff the next day was another Mexican standoff with all three finishing with 38. They turned for home and with each passing hole, Ouimet's play improved. Steadily he pulled ahead, and amidst complete disbelief and the great American enthusiasm, the boy from the caddy yard came home in 34 for a 72—five strokes

better than Vardon and six better than Ray. Almost overnight, America adopted Ouimet and golf. How complete has
been the adoption since then can be shown by simple figures. Few played the game prior to 1910—300,000 at best
—and today you have close to three million par chasers.
Ouimet supplied the initial impetus for this growth.

In that same 1913 Open at the Brookline Country Club,
another as yet unknown American competed. His name was
Walter Hagen and he came in fourth. Walter must be ranked
as another who did wonders for golf, both with his clubs
and his showmanship. He was a Barnum with golf sticks,
a colorful character who captured the fancy of people from
coast to coast.

"The Haig"—not to be confused with Haig and Haig—
won four British Opens, two U.S. Opens, five P.G.A. crowns
and a hatful of smaller tournaments, both here and abroad.
Blessed with steadfast faith in himself and a fantastic talent
to deliver in the clutch, Hagen was the most deceiving golfer
in the world. From start to finish, from tee to green, from
trap to rough, a round with Hagen took you on a tour of
a golf course. He was here, he was there, he always was in
trouble. But when somebody put a check on the line, he
would stand there and hole one out from a trap or drop a
wood shot dead on the green, inches from the cup.

The Haig's performance in the British Open in 1926,
played at the Royal–Lytham–St. Ann's course, was typical.
Pitted against the great Bobby Jones, Hagen needed an
eagle deuce on the last hole to tie the Atlanta shotmaker. An
eagle deuce, I don't have to tell you, is something you need
radar to get. That didn't bother The Haig as he reached the

last tee. Calmly, he slammed his first shot down the middle and it left him 150 yards from the pin. Now, to tie Jones, he had to hole his second shot—put it right smack in the cup from 150 yards out. He looked the situation over carefully, and then pulled a Babe Ruth. Strolling slowly from his ball to the green, surveying the distance, examining the green, he held the crowd's attention as if it was his opening night on Broadway. He looked back at his ball again, then turned to the referee. In a quiet voice he said, "Will you please remove the pin?" Then he left the stunned crowd and walked back 150 yards to his ball. Without a second glance he picked out his club and clobbered the ball right at the hole. It came down a bounce away from the cup, skipped straight for it —and then rolled over it, coming to rest only inches away on the other side. Haig had called an impossible shot and all but made it. His showmanship made an awful lot of people forget that he had missed and that Bobby Jones had won the tournament.

Before Hagen came along, in too many places a golf pro was nothing more than a lackey and used the servants' entrance at the club. England always was the pace setter in golf and the British custom called for pros, as a rule, to use the back door. But wherever Walter Hagen went, he went first class and the service he received, helped along by a twenty-dollar bill or a few pounds idly tossed on the table, was better than that granted an imperial potentate by his most servile subjects. Just as Grantland Rice made sports writing a first-rate profession with his genuine class, so did Hagen improve the lot of golf professionals. On his first English tour, he checked into the Ritz in London with a secretary and began the Hagen act. When interviewed by reporters, he left them awe-struck. They didn't know whether it was a golf pro or a king they had spoken with. He charmed them with his personality and knocked their eyes out with the splendor of his living. A few clubs, on his British tour, wouldn't allow him in their dining rooms. So he adopted the strategy of parking in front of these offending institutions in a Rolls Royce, where he had an elaborate picnic lunch served to him. The bars against golf pros were obliterated when Hagen came along and he has made the path a lot easier for the rest of us who followed.

I don't think there is a golf fan or player in the country who hasn't heard some yarn or other—and most of them are true—about The Haig's casual ways. This particular one has to do with Hagen's winning of the National P.G.A. at Salisbury Plains on Long Island in 1926. He was to meet Leo Diegel in a playoff and early that morning a friend of Hagen's was strolling on the lawn of the Garden City Hotel watching the dawn break. Out of the sunrise ambled The Haig coming back to his quarters after a night on the town.

"Diegel," the friend said accusingly, "has been in bed all night. Do you realize it is six in the morning?"

"Let him go to bed all night," Walter answered. "I'll bet he hasn't been sleeping well."

That afternoon Hagen went out and walloped Diegel five and three.

This game of golf took another leap upward when the one and only Robert Tyre Jones, Jr., came out of Atlanta, Georgia, to stalk the world's golf courses and compile the finest record of all—until Hogan. Bobby Jones came along in an era when the nation was sports-crazy. Babe Ruth was hitting home runs, Earl Sande was at the height of his turf career, Jack Dempsey was mauling opponents in the ring, and Red Grange was running wild on the gridiron. The Tildens, Nurmis, Paddocks, and Hitchcocks were performing magnificently, too, and the American people loved them all. This was sport's Golden Era, the fabulous ten years from 1923 until 1933. Golf needed somebody to carry its banner during this period and it certainly found the right man in Bobby Jones.

Bobby was a college-bred golfer and even today, down at his home diggings in Atlanta, he can show you sheepskins from Georgia Tech and Harvard. But he didn't learn his golf in school, for at the tender age of six The Emperor, as he later became known, was already swinging golf clubs, and at the age of eleven he won an Atlanta Athletic Club junior championship. Like Ouimet, Jones lived in a house no more than a chip shot from the East Lake Golf Course in Atlanta. A friendly golfer started him out by giving him a stick, an old cleek. Then a visiting Scottish pro, Stewart Maiden, took over for a year at East Lake and found a dogged little kid following him around the course and copying his "Carnoustie swing." Bobby copied it pretty well, too, for he still has it today. And so do a lot of other people who have copied Jones.

Jones retired from active tournament golf in 1930 at the early age of twenty-eight, but he left a record which stood unequaled until Ben Hogan hit his true stride a few years ago. Jones's 1930 accomplishments were enough to make people gasp. That year, playing as an amateur, a status he never gave up, he took the U.S. Open, the British Open, the U.S. Amateur, the British Amateur, and captained our winning Walker Cup team. Before 1930, he had run one-two in the U.S. Open for seven of the eight years, between 1923 and 1930, in which he played. He won it in 1923, 1925, 1926, 1929, and 1930.

People think that twenty-eight is still young for a golfer and register surprise when they realize that Jones retired at that age. But Bobby Jones was a tired veteran when he gave it up in 1930, exhausted physically and mentally from years of tournament golf. "There are two kinds of golf," he will tell you. "Golf and tournament golf. The latter is an aging game." Jones today is a successful lawyer and except for the illness which recently forced him to quit, would continue to play in one tournament each year—his own Masters at the Augusta Country Club in Atlanta.

If it can be said that Hogan resembles anyone in the golf world, he is most like Bobby Jones—in temperament and fortitude, anyway. In the National Open of 1923, held at the Inwood Country Club on Long Island, Bobby led the field by three strokes as the last round started. But coming home, he played miserably over the last four holes and blew sky-high on the eighteenth, taking a six. As he walked off the green, somebody remarked that it appeared the championship was his. Jones replied, "I didn't finish like a champion, I finished like a dog." Later, when informed that Bobby Cruickshank had tied him and a playoff was required, Bobby said, "The last hole Cruickshank played was one of the greatest in golf. It was also far and away the greatest for me. It gave me a chance to square myself." The next day, Jones went out and won on the nineteenth hole and took his first major title.

Jones's record is unbelievable, but no more so than Ben Hogan's when you put them side by side. Usually I don't like to refer to tables (they remind me of my income tax), but let's look at Jones's and Hogan's U.S. Open records. Below is a table comparing Hogan's last five performances in the U.S. Open with Jones's *best five*.

JONES			HOGAN		
Year	Course	Score	Year	Course	Score
1923	Inwood	296	1948	Riviera	276
1925	Worcester	291	1950	Merion	287
1926	Scioto	293	1951	Oakland Hills	287
1929	Winged Foot	294	1952	Northwood	286
1930	Interlachen	287	1953	Oakmont	283
		1461			*1419*

Hogan's total puts him 42 strokes ahead of Jones in Open play. Now I don't mean this to be one of those silly comparisons dreamed up to start an argument. It simply shows what each did on a total of ten golf courses, in different years, and under varying conditions. Jones's wooden shafts were inferior to Hogan's steel. Jones's courses were shorter and less manicured, Hogan's were longer and trickier. Not only courses and equipment but playing techniques have improved in twenty years. Competition is probably tougher today and opportunities for practice greater. In track, the time clock takes a further beating every year; in basketball the scores go higher; in football the passers become more accurate. It's the same story in golf. Par will take a worse licking next year, in all probability, than it did this. Some young fellow, today in diapers, will come along in 1975 and shoot scores which will make us all blink. Hogan himself feels the same way. "Ten years from now," he says, "the scores we shoot today will look silly. Control, concentration, discipline—you learn them through years of play. And somebody is learning right now." This mythical somebody is going to come down from the hills in 1975 and he'll take on Merion and play it in, say, 58. That's a prediction. Put it in your little black book.

Today it's relatively easy to find out how Hogan plays golf. There are books, movies, television features—just about every information outlet you can think of—to teach up-and-coming golfers how Hogan and other pros do it. We never had these aids when I was a caddy learning the game. But, now, on any golf course, you meet people who say, "Hogan does it this way; I'll try it too." Maybe they don't come close to emulating his game, maybe they have no idea what the man does. But in the future, just as we have seen it happen in the past, more people will learn the fundamentals correctly as youngsters and then step up to the tee and put par in a coffin.

It is not necessary to confine the comparison to just Bobby Jones. Hogan has outshot every great score recorded by the old-timers. Ty Cobb's performance in the world of baseball is an illustration in reverse of the same point. Cobb stole a million bases and took all the liberties in the world on both outfielders and catchers. But if Ty were playing today, with gents like Carl Furillo throwing them in from the outfield and a Yogi Berra or Roy Campanella behind the plate, he would be keeping his feet much closer to that bag.

The techniques of stopping a runner from taking an extra base have improved so much that it would be suicide to try today what Cobb got away with thirty years ago.

Hogan's influence in golf is going to extend far beyond just low scores in the U.S. Open. It was this point that I was thinking about as I rode up New York City's Broadway in the ticker-tape parade for Hogan that August day in 1953 he arrived back in America after taking the British Open on his first try. There were all sorts of celebrities and a whole mob of newspaper friends waiting at the dock for the S.S. *United States* to arrive with the little man from Fort Worth. When we reached New York's City Hall, Mayor Vincent Impellitteri made a speech ("Here you are, the world's greatest golfer and here I am, the world's worst") and presented a scroll to Ben. As he did, I looked around in amazement at the huge crowd in front of the reception stand, straining for a look at Hogan. I turned to Toots Shor, the New York restaurant man and America's No. 1 sports fan, and asked him, "Toots, how many of those people out here do you think ever had a golf club in their hands?"

"Less than a quarter of them," he replied. "But they'll be out on a driving range or buying clubs this week end."

I was thinking precisely the same thing. Ben's performance was making converts right and left. I look for golf to enter a new phase with these Hogan triumphs. We've had the Feather Ball, the Gutta Percha Ball, and the Rubber Ball Periods. We've had Ouimet, Hagen, Gene Sarazen, Jones, and Byron Nelson. Now we are in the middle of the Hogan Period. Golf is going to make tremendous strides during Ben's time of prominence.

Golf is a game which goes a long way toward bridging the gap between a strictly spectator and a participation sport. There have been a lot of complaints going the rounds about the way the automobile and the grandstand seat, and now television, have reduced the American male to a soft type of character. Some of these ideas may have substance. A seat behind home plate for three hours of baseball never did a thing for a man's physique; 6 inches of board on the 50-yard line is made to order for an expanding posterior.

But golf, I've always felt, is the answer to growing old. You don't have to be a tournament professional, you don't even have to be young and in training, to enjoy the game. Even if you kick the ball around with your foot, the very fact that you walk a pleasant eighteen holes and use some of those dormant muscles and get some fresh air in your lungs is enough. It does more for you than a membership card in six different kinds of health clubs.

Now don't get me wrong. I'm not knocking the spectator sports. Baseball is a game I truly love and when I get a chance to take in a major-league ball game, I'm one of the first persons in the park. But people should have some outlet for physical energy and some way of keeping in condition. For my few dollars, golf is it.

The age factor is important too. Tennis players, ball-players, track men, boxers—they're all ancient at thirty-five. Ben is forty-three years old and he can still beat any breathing human being from six to sixty who wants to challenge him with golf sticks. This fact has shaken up a lot of the rocking-chair set and sent them out to golf courses. President

Eisenhower is sixty-three, and every time he steps out onto a course his game improves.

I see this influence at work on my own Concord International course at Kiamesha Lake, New York. Day in and day out, since the Hogan victories, people who never played golf before, and probably considered themselves too old to start, come walking into my shop and ask me, "Where does a beginner go to learn?"

This boom should have a chain reaction right through the entire business. It should stop the alarming trend which saw people selling their beautiful greens and fairways for housing developments. It is going to reach the equipment manufacturers, too. The heavier demand the future will bring is bound to introduce more mass production into golf. And when it comes, millions of Sunday golfers will find their golf dollars going a lot farther.

One place this boom will touch heavily is our source of top playing pros. The boys up there today, the Sam Sneads, Hogans, Jackie Burkes, Lloyd Mangrums, all began their careers as caddies. The same is true in my own case. Nobody ever toted around more bags than Jimmy Demaret. I'll match shoulder creases with any man alive. But in the future it's going to be different. Instead of a boy having to spend his time around a golf course to learn the game, the U.S. Open champ twenty years from now is going to be a college graduate with a major letter in golf from some fine university. The game is destined to become an important college activity. Schools around the country right now have golf teams, but it's still considered a minor sport. This situation is already changing. The University of North Carolina has a beautiful golf layout right off its campus at Chapel Hill, and many other institutions are in the process of building them. The United States Military Academy at West Point also has a course adjacent to its campus.

I'm not the only one who holds this view. There's a famous weeping Irishman out at South Bend, Indiana, who will tell you the same thing—Frank Leahy, former football coach at Notre Dame. He said a while back, "We now have more Notre Dame boys going out for the golf team than we do for football. Judging from the number of people playing golf, I guess it isn't such a strange thing."

To be quite frank, money never hurts, either. Those little green coupons which rustle around in your jeans aren't exactly going to kill the game. The prize for winning a major tournament today is enough to make even an old fellow like Demaret practice. A man can open a pretty good bank account if he wins such as the Tam O'Shanter World Open, where promoter George May puts up $120,000 in prize money. For proof you need look no farther than Hogan. He's won everything in sight in the past thirteen years. I understand that when he walks into the bank at Fort Worth, the president himself gets behind the window to handle his business.

It's a far cry from the windy day in 1934 when J. Demaret came in first in the Texas P.G.A. Tournament at Dallas—a win for which I received the princely sum of $25. I was the leading money winner for the week, too. It's a lot different today, however. A top tournament pro can earn somewhere in the neighborhood of $50,000, in prizes and in subsidiary income, if he has a good year and stays up there with the leaders.

Golf galleries used to be unheard-of. In fact, when I was a boy, anybody who practiced golf or talked about it in football-whacky Houston was considered a sissy. But at the U.S. Open this year, there were 28,000 out on the last day, giving the event an average attendance of 25,000 for the three-day whirl. And over at Carnoustie, they turned out from every place this side of New Zealand. Of course Hogan was the main event. He had 20,000 people in his own gallery over the last few holes. Ben has the same drawing power over here, too. The first American exhibition he played after his British triumph—eighteen relaxed holes at a course in Jamesburg, New Jersey—brought out 8,000 people. They mobbed the place just to see Hogan play eighteen holes that didn't count.

An important part of golf's financial future is going to be the thing that has hurt a lot of other sports—television, that face on your living-room wall. It doesn't take a business genius to foresee the day when big sponsors will pay heavy cash so that their wide-angled cameras can catch just as much of a golf match as a football or basketball game. Irving Mansfield, one of the television industry's top producers, says that "when the day comes that a golf match can be properly picked up by a television camera—and it's certainly going to come—the winner of the U.S. Open will pick up one of the largest individual purses in professional sports." Golf is a game played by so many today that it should be a terrific TV hit when videoed on a grand scale. The presence of the camera eye on the course could insure an enormous payday for big tournament winners.

Of course we all hope that TV doesn't cut down on the average crowd of 25,000 now watching our major matches. Hogan, who at one time just couldn't stand being near too many people, has grown entirely accustomed to large galleries and actually enjoys their presence. Besides, galleries have produced a lot of the laughs you get on a golf course, and laughs are made to order for tense, overwrought human beings in hot competition. Once, when I was playing in the Goodall Round Robin at Wykagil, I came out on the course in a pair of chartreuse slacks, an orange shirt and checkered tam. The tourney is sponsored by the Palm Beach people, so I guess the crowd was clothes-conscious. Anyway, as I was waiting to tee off on number four I felt a hand stroking my trousers. I looked around, in a hurry, and there was a woman who had broken sixty some years ago and with no trouble.

"Young man," she said, "do you mind if I feel your trousers?"

I don't think anybody had ever said yes to her before, but I nodded in a confused kind of way. When she got through, she turned around and screamed at the top of her scratchy voice, "It's charmeen, Mabel. Just like I said!"

Her scream coincided with Jackie Burke's backswing and caused him to top his ball badly. I picked up the hole and ultimately two points. Ever since, Mabel's friend has remained my favorite clothes connoisseur.

The fickle attitude of a golf gallery is something which you just have to get used to. Those people are strictly for the

American way of doing things: in sports, never stick too long with a loser. Dr. Cary Middlecoff, the Memphis dentist who finds golf more exciting, tells about the crowd with him on his first tournament after he won the Open in 1949. Cary had more than a thousand people in his own private gallery when he started out, but it just wasn't to be a good day for him. He was working on a big 78—which left him six strokes off the leaders—and along about the tenth hole, people started deserting him and heading for the boys with the lower scores. When Cary reached the eighteenth, he started up the fairway with a gallery consisting of "my two opponents, three caddies, and some guy who was in the Army with me and wanted to borrow ten bucks."

CHAPTER 3

THE EARLY DAYS

In the long and hallowed history of golf, I don't think anybody has held a championship by a wider margin than Ben Hogan and I. Through the 1930s, we were consistent winners in the Lean and Low Tournament, which means we had little weight and less money. If two broker guys ever started out in golf, we've never heard of them. Possible contestants for the championship wisely dropped off by the wayside and took jobs in diners and on road gangs.

I'm pretty proud of the fact that I share this title. No matter how you slice it, it's a good thing for a man to be able to say he made his own way in this world. And we overcame a fair number of obstacles to do it. It always gives me a great laugh when somebody refers to golf as a rich man's game. My wife, who remembers the lean and hungry days only too well, agrees that golf isn't only for millionaires. We were at a party last winter and "Red" leaned over and gave me a nice wifely kiss and said aloud that she thought her husband was—well, an adequate performer. You know how wives talk.

44

"You're just saying that because he has money," somebody said.

"I told him the same thing when he didn't have a quarter —and I mean a quarter," she answered. She wasn't kidding. When I was broke, I was just what that word means. And in those days nobody could spare a dime even for their best buddy.

Hogan came from exactly the same setup, but today Ben doesn't like to talk too much about those early years. Since he's hit the top, people from all over have been asking him about his early background, and he seems inclined to shrug most of the questions off. A lot of inquisitive folks go away with the feeling that he doesn't want anybody to know he ever was any place but on top. I don't think that's the reason. In my opinion Ben just doesn't want to be reminded of the early days. Some periods of a person's life are just too unpleasant to talk about. He's probably put those memories away in the "file and forget" department. But I have a pretty good idea that once in a while, Ben will lift a Scotch and soda in some expensive bistro, look around him, and say to himself, "Pretty good for a kid from Texas who started out selling papers."

William Benjamin Hogan was born in Dublin, Texas, a small cattle town about 75 miles from Fort Worth, on (he says) August 13, 1912. I was born in 1910 and I know Ben is a year older than I am. But I think a man, once he's turned the corner of thirty-nine, is entitled to set his own age as long as he's reasonable about it. Ben's father, Chester Hogan, was the town blacksmith and junk dealer. Dublin is aptly named, because it is an Irish settlement, stuck in the middle of the

Texas plains. One entire block of the little town, in Ben's time, was inhabited by Hogans and Gallaghers. Ben was one of three children. He has an older brother, Royal, with whom he is a partner in a Fort Worth office-equipment business today, and a sister who is married. It was just a normal small-town life for Ben until he was nine years old. Then his father became ill, and on a bleak February day Ben and his mother had to drive Chester Hogan to Fort Worth and put him in a hospital, where he died shortly afterward. When the shock wore off, the family left Dublin—where there weren't many ways a woman with three children could support her family —and moved to Fort Worth for good.

The larger city offered no rosy prospects, but the family managed to make ends meet. Ben and Royal had to hustle newspapers to help pay the bills at home. Ben, with the kind of drive and determination we've come to expect of him today, put everything he had into selling his bundle of papers. Many nights he stayed out until after midnight, meeting the late trains at Fort Worth's Union Station and making his sales. For a kid of ten or eleven years, such late hours were not healthy. "I was skinny and small and I wasn't getting much sleep between selling papers and trying to go to school," Ben says. "I don't think it did me any good." Perhaps those long evenings on street corners during his growing years have a lot to do with his being on the smallish side today. As a matter of fact he was even smaller when he started out in golf.

The Hogan family's move from Dublin to Fort Worth is important if for no other reason than it introduced Ben to golf. There were no courses around Dublin, but Fort Worth had several, and when he was twelve, Ben began haunting golf courses instead of selling papers. He had heard about this business called caddying and decided to try it. The common tale is that Ben went out to the Glen Garden Country Club and began to pack bags with another Fort Worth kid, Byron Nelson. That yarn became a golf promoter's dream in the 1940s when Hogan and Nelson faced each other in exciting contests all over the country. Actually, Ben first packed a bag at a little nine-hole sand greens course on the south side of town named Katy Lake, which is no longer in existence today. This decision by a twelve-year-old to give up the newspaper business (I'm sure that with his determination Hogan would be publisher of a string of Texas newspapers today if he'd stuck at it) was to pay fat dividends to the world of golf a quarter of a century later.

In those depression days, a caddy got 65 cents a round and the rounds were far from plentiful. Naturally, a newcomer to the caddy yard was treated with suspicion and, if he showed a little hesitation, was given the bum's rush by the other boys and tossed out. A new caddy meant fewer rounds and fees for the rest of the bag-toters and they did their best to guard against competition. When Ben, a scrawny half-pint twelve-year-old, showed up, he was given the works. The rest of the caddies went into a huddle, and, with the special kind of cruelty only kids can dream up, shoved forward the biggest boy to test Ben's qualifications. "Fight him and lick him if you want to loop [caddy] around here," they said.

Then some of the more imaginative of these juvenile delinquents had a better idea for getting rid of this skinny

47

newcomer. They grabbed an old barrel standing in the caddy yard, tossed Ben into it, and sent it rolling down a steep rocky hill behind the yard, with Ben inside. It crashed against a rock at the bottom and most of the staves were broken. When the little kid crawled out, he felt as if his ribs had caved in. That was enough, the older boys figured, to scare away this newcomer. But when you have to work in order to eat, and you have a strong hankering to leave newspapers and street corners for the inviting green outdoors of a golf course, it takes more than a rough trip downhill in a barrel to scare you off. Ben Hogan had a job to do and he started back up the hill looking for that big kid. He battled the older boy with such tenacity and grim determination that almost immediately his opponent was looking for a way out and the rest of the caddies were getting ready to accept this bantam rooster into the sacred fraternity of the caddy yard.

Today, when they write about the grim determination Hogan shows in a golf tournament, they make it seem like a trait recently acquired. "Battling Ben," they call him. Actually, a man never really learns to take things easy after he starts life off in the manner Ben Hogan did. There were schools in Texas—even in those days—but Ben didn't have much time for studying, although he did attend Central High in Fort Worth briefly. Eating took precedence over culture, like it or not.

The first time Hogan took a swing at a golf ball it was with an old rusty driver. It happened to be a left-handed club, so Ben simply turned himself around and learned to bang the ball southpaw style. At that time he was packing bags for that enormous 65 cents an hour at the Glen Garden course in Fort Worth. His fellow caddies there had a little game which may have had something to do with establishing his early practice habits. The game was called "shag," and under its rules, the caddies would line up, ten at a time, and hit balls. The unlucky one with the shortest drive would have to go out and retrieve for all the others. This took precious time which could be better spent packing bags for the paying customers. Also, the loser took an unmerciful ribbing from the rest of the gang. Smaller or no, Ben just had to learn how to hit that ball at least as far as the next guy.

His answer then, as a twelve-year-old novice caddy, was the same answer he applies to golf problems today—practice. First, he enlisted the aid of Ted Longworth, the Glen Garden pro, who let him use a right-handed club and convinced him that he'd get more distance from his natural side. Ben agreed to turn around, but he began by holding the club cross-handed, his left hand under the right. We call that cow-handed in Texas. "I was pretty good at it, too," Hogan recalls today. Longworth took him under his wing again and straightened out his grip, but Ben still had that firm left hand and he's never lost it.

As you might guess, those older caddies soon were spending a lot of time picking up Hogan's drives. Yet despite those hours of practice, Denny Lavender, who grew up around Glen Garden and went on to become the golf instructor at the United States Military Academy, remembers Ben as one of the poorest-looking golf prospects he'd seen. "He didn't do one single thing right in those days," Denny recalls.

There was one caddy who could do nothing wrong on the golf course at Glen Garden. That was Byron Nelson, who was occasionally breaking 70 even in those days. Nelson was the lad they considered the golfer with the future around Fort Worth. But Hogan continued to grind out those practice sessions. With the grim face of a man fifteen years his senior, Ben would go out on the course after his day's work and hit hours of golf balls. His determination paid off in a Christmas Day caddy tournament in the middle 1920s in which Ben tied Byron Nelson in a big local upset. "I guess that was one of my first big achievements with a golf stick," Ben says today. "After it was over, the other caddies went to a Christmas party. But I felt that I'd already had my party when I tied Nelson." Even today, his outlook is much the same. Instead of going to the party with the rest of us after a tough round, he often picks up his sticks and heads for the course and a little two-hour practice session. "If you can't outplay them, outwork them." That's always been his slogan.

While Hogan was selling papers, toting bags, and learning the game in those early years, there was a young boy downstate in Houston who was facing many of the same problems. I, James Demaret, hail from a big family of Dutch-Irish stock. My father, John O'Brien Demaret, was a carpenter, roofer, house painter, and general building tradesman. That's a decent living, and my mother was proud of my dad's profession. But no matter what you bring home from a week's work, it isn't enough when there are nine children in the family. My mother, we were sometimes reminded, used to serve thirty-three meals a day when we were all at home. I was one of five boys, and at one time or another we were all selling papers. Believe me, Houston has bought a lot of papers from the Demaret brothers. At the ripe old age of eight years, I was the best newspaper pusher that ever played hooky from the third grade. I'd camp at a bus stop in the middle of town and begin chanting, "It's murder! It's murder!" People would literally leap at me to buy papers and after scanning the front page would ask, "What's murder?" In a low voice I would answer, "The heat, mister . . . the heat." Usually I'd get away with it. Papers only cost two cents in those days and it was a rare villain who would get rough with an eight-year-old kid over two cents.

One fateful day, I walked past the Camp Logan army hospital golf course, which was near my home. I stayed around for a few minutes and watched the wounded soldiers —World War I had just ended—knocking golf balls around. At this time, the only two sports that interested me were baseball and football; in fact I was determined to become a big-league baseball player. Golf sounded, and looked, like a crazy game to me—until one of the neighborhood kids told me you could make money carrying bags for the soldiers. That made it look a little less crazy.

Pretty soon I was seeing more of that nine-hole course than the greenskeeper. I forgot about peddling newspapers and took up caddying with a vengeance. Then one afternoon an army doctor handed me a beat-up pitching iron. Proudly I walked over to a corner of the course, took a few swings— and I was a slave for life. The golf bug had taken its toll. I swung that rusty iron, and any other club I could get my hands on, until the course closed, day in and day out. When I was eleven, I won my first caddy tournament on that same

Camp Logan course with a sizzling 86. From Camp Logan, I moved over to the public golf course at Hermann Park, Houston, and stayed there until I was twelve years old.

I don't claim that caddying is the very best way for a kid to start out in life. In a caddy yard I saw a lot of things which proved somewhat alarming—knife fights, sharp gambling, plain robbery. It's golf's version of the School of Hard Knocks—not altogether an easy life but certainly educational. But only a few of my experiences in the caddy yard were ugly ones. I made lifelong friends there, and met many older men genuinely interested in the game.

From caddying, I moved into the golf shop at Hermann Park and worked on building up my forearms. People sometimes ask me today how I obtained my wrist and forearm development. The answer is simple—from my weekly chore of buffing 350 sets of clubs that had been hacked and chipped over the week end by members. Also, I was a member of that last generation of golf pros which served a rugged apprenticeship making and mending those wooden shafts, just before the mass factory production of clubs began. I was listed as an "apprentice clubmaker" at Hermann Park and was able to fill the job because my father had schooled me well in the handling of tools. I learned the techniques of making and mending the hickory shafts thoroughly, and most any hour of the day I could be found pressing them against the shop lathe.

After four years at Hermann Park, I moved over to the Golfcrest Country Club and then on to the Colonial Country Club and finally to Houston's River Oaks Club where I went to work for a man who has been a favorite of mine ever since, Jack Burke, Sr. Under Burke, I was made caddy master and starter, with the job of baby-sitting with Jack Burke, Jr., thrown in. I never really did get away from that job, either. Today Jackie is a member of my staff at the Concord Hotel.

From his caddy days, Ben Hogan matured steadily into a player who caught the eye of the discerning few. He never did win an amateur title—he lost in the finals of the Fort Worth city tournament when sixteen—but the long drives he was able to hit, despite his small size, and those night-and-day practice sessions impressed those who stopped for a second look. One such impressed spectator was Ted Longworth, the Glen Garden pro who first persuaded Hogan to hit from the right side. Ted, who retired last year from active duty as head pro at the Waverley Country Club in Portland, Oregon, took Ralph Guldahl and Hogan to a local tournament at St. Louis in 1931, an overnight hop from Fort Worth.

When the three arrived in St. Louis, a Joplin, Missouri, golf writer asked Longworth who the two youngsters were. Ben was only nineteen at the time. "They're a couple of real good kids," Ted answered. "Guldahl is ready to go now, but the younger one—this Hogan—might take it all someday." Guldahl finished in the money in that tournament and then went on to win the Phoenix Open that year and finish second in the U.S. Open the next. Longworth was right on his first prophecy. But he had to wait several years before his prediction about Hogan was proved to be a brilliant one.

"Ben's success is no particular surprise to me," Longworth

says. "I remember the day I told him he'd never make a golfer as a southpaw. He listened to me closely and then he said, 'Sure!' He asked a couple of intelligent questions and went away. I didn't figure he'd paid much attention. But the next time I saw him, he was chopping away cow-handed and getting a lot more distance. I corrected him on that, and then he put in more time on a normal grip and swing. Pretty soon he was hammering the ball out of sight. I guess I was the first person to tout Hogan around the nation. At least as far out of Fort Worth as St. Louis."

After his unsuccessful debut in St. Louis, Ben tried a few other tournaments in 1931, but the results were not spectacular. He won $50 at Phoenix and $87.50 at San Antonio and ultimately arrived at the Los Angeles Open with exactly 15 cents left in his jeans.

This was the beginning of the lean years on the golf circuit for determined Ben Hogan. From 1931 until 1940, *he won only one tournament*. Time and again he found himself completely without money and, on a lot of occasions, without hope. It was a long and discouraging haul for Ben and would have spelled complete defeat for a lesser man. He'd skimp and deprive himself in order to make a tournament—and then finish out of the money. They began to call Ben "The Perennial Also-Ran," and it got so that he believed it himself. "Am I always going to finish just out of the money? Can't I ever get a win for myself?" I heard him ask such questions many times during this period.

When he reached Los Angeles in 1931 with that handsome 15 cents, he proceeded to finish out of the money again. It looked as if tournament golf was simply out of Ben's reach. He lived mostly on fruit through the Los Angeles event and then had to wire a friend in Fort Worth for funds on which to come home. He went back with his old boss, Ted Longworth, who had become part owner of the Oakhurst public course a few miles outside of Fort Worth.

Working at Longworth's course was no gold mine either. "Few people ever came out there to play," Ben recalls, "but it did one thing for me. I could practice four hours every morning. I started off by chipping for an hour or so and then I'd move back and work on my wood shots. Then I'd putt." During his nonpractice time, Ben's only revenue came from selling golf balls to a well-heeled foursome that played Longworth's course regularly. These same gents would back Ben in a match with anyone who came along and, if he won it, cut him in on the profit.

As soon as he had saved a little, Ben would hit the tour again. The little man was working hard at it when I went on my first tour late in 1934 with Lew Nash, Ed Beedle Juelg, and Ted Menefee, now the pro at the San Antonio Country Club. Ben was barnstorming with Ralph Guldahl and Byron Nelson and between the seven of us, except for Nelson, I don't think we won enough to pay breakfast bills. But despite his many defeats, Hogan was continually improving his game. He had no money to spend while he was on tour, so he put all his free time into practice. He and Nelson would spend hour after hour on the practice tee, something unheard-of in those days. The old-timers in golf rarely practiced. They'd take a few swings to limber up and then go out and play in a tournament. Hogan and Nelson began almost a new concept with those lengthy practice sessions.

The 1934 tour was a lush one for Jimmy Demaret. Everything strictly first-class. It began at Houston, when I approached the late Charley Schwartz, a caddy, and made a brilliant deal with him. "Charley, if you'll caddy for me at the Texas P.G.A. at Dallas, I'll give you half of what I win." Charley okayed the proposition and the career of James Demaret, tournament pro, was off to a spectacular start. Why was I so particular about bringing a caddy of my own with me? That's simple. I couldn't afford to pay for one at the tournament. And carrying my own clubs was against the rules. Anyway, as the Orientals put it, I couldn't afford to lose face.

So Charley and I took off for Dallas and the Texas P.G.A. in the best and fastest first-class freight we could find. It was a Missouri, Kansas and Texas Railroad special. We hopped it at Houston at nine o'clock on a Tuesday night, our complete baggage consisting of two clean shirts and a single toothbrush. We found ourselves in the comfortable confines of a boxcar half loaded with fruit. We sprawled casually on the floor, using small piles of oranges and grapefruits for pillows, but a Texas night in February can be a bit cool and this particular one was frigid. We were just about freezing when Charley decided to close up the reefers which had been left open to allow the fruit proper ventilation. Frankly, we didn't care too much about the fruit. As we merrily battened down hatches, a railroad detective, walking along the top of the train, heard the noise and came down for a look, with that big club in his hand. He swung into the car and saw us. I began to talk a bit, but Charley had the right idea. He grabbed the clubs and jumped. I followed him, clutching

Another enthusiastic golfer, President Dwight D. Eisenhower, studies Ben's grip at the White House, August 8, 1953. Ben's wife Valerie looks on (*Wide World Photos*).

Two of America's foremost golfers, Bobby Jones and Ben Hogan, talk over the golf picture in 1953 (*Wide World Photos*).

Ben and his wife Valerie. She stays constantly in the background and is rarely interviewed or photographed (*Wide World Photos*).

the little bag with our two shirts. Luckily the train was poking along and we landed more or less on our feet.

Another train with proper accommodations (an empty boxcar) came by eventually and when we arrived in Dallas at a late hour we casually informed our fellow golfers that "our train was delayed." We checked in, a bit jauntily, I thought, at the Hotel Waco and immediately had a room-service meal, signing a check for it. As we had arrived in town with exactly nothing in our pockets, it seemed to me that these expenses were a bit out of line. But Charley was hungry and he convinced me that I was hungry too and that everything would turn out for the best. He was right; I was a great success in the tournament. My shots were steady and I held doggedly to the lead after the first day. It was the same story the second day out and then I rode home with two fine rounds the last day to set a new record of 286, capture first place, *and win the magnificent sum of $25.*

On the way back to the hotel, Charley and I mulled over our troubles. We agreed that the $25 was our get-home money and that it wasn't going to help us any if we paid the hotel bill. So he waited outside with the clubs, under the window of our fourth-floor room, and I went upstairs and packed our meager belongings. Then I leaned out the window and dropped them to Charley. He didn't miss a thing. Wally Shang's catch of a baseball tossed off the Washington Monument was nothing compared to Charley's performance that day underneath the fourth-floor window of the Hotel Waco. Then I nonchalantly walked downstairs empty-handed and past the old lady behind the counter. "Still have to play some more?" she asked in what I took to be a suspicious tone. She probably was just being pleasant. "Yeah," I sighed. "Have to play a tough round tomorrow. I just want to take a few minutes' walk."

But the winner of the Texas P.G.A. and his personal caddy didn't walk. We took the regular train back to Houston and enjoyed every mile of it. As a postscript to this story, I might add that two years later, I sent the Waco Hotel a check and a note of explanation. Ever since, I've considered them old friends who helped me out when I most needed it.

After my Dallas success, I went to the Galveston Municipal Course as pro and began to frequent the Hollywood Dinner Club in that town. In those days, Sam Maceo, who owned it, was bringing in the big-name bands of the day, and my passion for popular music would get completely out of hand whenever Glen Gray or George Olsen or Ben Bernie and their bands would come through. Then, as now, I'd jump up on the stand and croon a ballad or two with the orchestra, if given even the slightest encouragement. My vocal talents, such as they were, made enough of an impression on Bernie so that he offered me a job and I was seriously considering it. But Maceo, a big-time operator of the day and also a golf enthusiast, ridiculed the suggestion. "You want to be a golfer. Why mess around with singing? You swing good enough for me. Why don't you make the tour?" I then gave him the stock answer of those penniless days—"With what?" His reply was enough money for me to get together once again with Nash, Juelg, and Menefee. Thus I was saved at the last moment from the terrible fate of a Bing Crosby.

This particular tour I still refer to as the Ry-Krisp Circuit. It was the shortest cut to slenderizing I've ever known. We hit every tournament in California and, spending our money dime by dime, slowly approached that disheartening "broke point." However, I broke the spell by taking a third in the Sacramento Open and winning $385. It seemed like a million dollars to me then. But in order to subsist while the tournament was still in progress, the four of us, Nash, Juelg, Menefee, and myself, had to do what Ben and others had done before us—rely mostly on oranges. We were playing over Riverside's Victoria Golf Course, and around the boundaries of this course there are trees loaded down with those juicy California navel oranges. In practice rounds, playing along the ninth hole, one of us would take careful aim and shoot into the trees. The shot would go out of bounds and cost a stroke, but it was a necessary sacrifice. On the pretext of hunting for the ball (a valuable item in 1934) we would forage in the orange grove, filling our stomachs and even our golf bags with the wonderful fruit. Often this was the next morning's breakfast as well as the evening's dinner.

From Sacramento, $385 richer, we went to Frisco and then to Oakmont and finally to Agua Caliente, where I picked up a $750 prize for a third-place tie. I had arrived! I had tasted the delights of the big money as well as the juice of pilfered oranges.

Hogan on this tour didn't win a cent. Ben was playing good golf, but he couldn't buy a putt and too often his drives were going haywire. At this stage, Ben was slamming the ball in a low, right-to-left trajectory and the habit was getting him into a lot of trouble. Ben was a terrific hitter—in my opinion, he slammed the ball harder then than he does now—but his habit of hitting low, screaming drives and his putting difficulty were proving costly. His putter became an obsession with him. He practiced literally night and day with the stick. As for his drives, in later years Ben was to learn the left-to-right fade with his woods (an important technicality explained fully in Chapter 8), and it steadied his game to a considerable extent.

But on that 1934 tour, Ben tried just about every trick in the book, but he couldn't win a thing. His severe case of financial destitution didn't help him, either. Today, whenever we talk over those early years, Ben will remember one thing. "Remember what you could get to eat in a diner in those days, Jimmy?" Then he looks at me, wistful-like. "For fifteen cents—just fifteen cents—I used to order two eggs, sausage, potatoes and toast and coffee. It was terrific food, too."

When Ben came off that tour, he made a move which I am positive has been a major factor in his career as a professional golfer. He married Valerie Fox, a girl he had met at Sunday school back in Dublin when he was about twelve and had known ever since. Valerie is a girl who is blessed with strong insight and sure knowledge of what her husband needs from her. In my opinion Valerie has been one of Ben's secret weapons ever since. She is as fine a woman as it has been my privilege to meet.

Now that he was a married man with responsibilities, Ben gave up the golf tour. His ambition to make the top still burned in him, but there was no corresponding lucre burning a hole in his pocket. Ben worked at several jobs around Fort Worth. He was a busboy at a restaurant and an attendant at a garage. Then a chance came along for him to take a "stick man's" job at a Fort Worth gaming house. His brief career as a croupier is one particular facet of Hogan's life you can't get Ben even to whisper about today. For some reason, he goes out of his way to prevent it being mentioned. Why he feels this way I don't know, but I can say one thing for sure: he has nothing to be ashamed of. Some of my best friends are croupiers and some of my best money has been lost over the dice and roulette tables. Ben was a hungry kid with no money and a wife. The job came and he took it. Today he must certainly be ranked among the most honest people in golf. He would call a penalty on himself for some minor infraction even if he was standing all alone in the middle of the Sahara Desert.

Perhaps the story of the late Bill Klem, the father of modern baseball umpiring, is one Ben should take to heart. Klem always said he never made a bad call in his career—in his heart. And he meant it. There was nobody with more scruples than old Bill. But he played the horses and played them pretty well, or so the story goes. So well and so often that the late Judge Landis, baseball's commissioner, called him in to talk the matter over.

"They say you bet on races with bookmakers," Landis observed.

"That's right, Judge, I do," Klem snorted. "And I pay one hundred cents on the dollar when I lose and they pay me one hundred cents on the dollar when I win." That ended the interview. Klem had nothing to hide and Judge Landis realized it.

Now I'm not saying that Ben enjoyed the gambling business. In all probability he didn't. His whole approach to life would have prevented his liking the job. But knowing Ben and his insistence on perfection, I would hazard a guess that he took the stick home at night and practiced with it on the dining-room table. . . . But I'd probably best drop the subject. In another minute I'll be telling you about the time I made seven passes in a row at Las Vegas.

While Ben stayed home at Fort Worth and tried to scrape together enough money to live on, and to save a few dollars for another crack at the tour, Demaret had another fling at being an itinerant golf pro. In December of 1935 Jack Grout, who is now the professional at Sioda Country Club in Columbus, Ohio, agreed to pool his money with mine (which was exactly nothing) and afterward we would split any winnings we made on the tour (which came to even less). We began at Pasadena, finished out of the money, and then blandly decided to enter the Catalina Open on Catalina Island. We traveled there with that same what-can-they-do-to-us? air that Charley Schwartz and I adopted in Dallas in 1934. We checked into the classy Santa Catalina Hotel even though we were a bit low on cash.

The first day at Catalina I got a break. It rained all day and I had a chance to sit down with Bill Melhorn, a fine player of that period and an early idol of mine. I loved to talk golf with Bill, but more important at this stage, Bill wanted to play checkers. I'm not the greatest shark in the world at checkers or cards or any other such tranquil occupation. I can't sit still long enough to finish a round. But this was different. We were playing for a dollar a game. I pulled up a chair in the hotel lobby, tensed every muscle to stay awake, and applied all my powers of concentration. I must have looked like a cigar-store Indian behind a checkerboard. I didn't move a muscle all that afternoon and right through a large part of the night. All my moves were made on the checkerboard, and I beat Melhorn out of enough to pay the hotel bill. You can't imagine what a fine clean feeling it was for me in those days—being able to walk past the house detective without having to worry about his gently inquiring if I had enough to pay the bill.

When the Catalina Open began, it quickly became apparent that my golf was not in the same class with my checker playing. I moved myself right out of competition with some of the flashiest over-par golf you ever saw. Grout, however, remained in a pretty good position and on the last day had a fair chance of finishing among the top five or six. Now Jack had been playing golf strictly for fun on this tour. His attitude bewildered me. He didn't know what a golf purse looked like and he didn't seem to care. On this last day of the tournament, I went out with him, acting as sort of a fore-caddy and trying to pull him through to that nice prize money we would split fifty-fifty. He was three strokes under par as we started on the last eighteen and I was already counting the spoils.

Demaret the psychologist went to work. I thought I'd calm him down a little. "Now, Jack, I think if you just shoot par from here on you'll be okay. Settle down, play a steady game, and you have a fine chance to win some money for us here."

Jack turned around and looked at me blankly. In those days he stuttered, but never this badly. "We—we—we p-p-playing f-f-for mon—m-m-m-money?" he gasped.

Old Jack's knees sagged. Then he pulled himself together and went out and shot more bogies than I've ever seen in a single round. He finished up with an immaculate card—not a par or birdie on it—and a score of 89. We went back to the hotel with empty hands and emptier stomachs.

During the 1936 tour, Hogan stuck it out at Fort Worth and Demaret played with the losers on the tournament trail. But Ben was getting his spirits and his funds in order for a big try in 1937. I hadn't seen Ben since the '34 tour and spent a little time talking with the Hogans—he had Valerie with him now—at the General Brock Open at Niagara Falls, New York, in May of 1937.

"I've got the secret of this game now," I remember Ben telling me. He and Valerie had left Fort Worth in a battered car, with the carefully hoarded sum of about $825 in their kick. But if Ben had found "the secret" at that time, he lost it again immediately. It was the same story, and a heart-breaking one, for the Hogans. Ben tied for eleventh in the General Brock, he came in ninth in the Shawnee Open, he placed ninth in the Glens Falls Open. And so it went.

Ben and Valerie reached Oakland, California, in late February of 1937, with $5 in the family coffers. Grimly, Ben went out to the course and worked until dusk made it impossible for him to see his practice shots. This was the make-or-break test for the little man. He knew only too well that he must win in Oakland or they would have to go home once again. For the early tournaments, he and Val had lived on hamburgers, but after a while their money even for those was running out. "If I don't win here, we'll sell the car and go home," Ben promised his wife.

The Hawk played it carefully for the first two days at Oakland. He stayed in contention and it looked as if he had a chance, going into the last day, to finish well in the money. But his putting still was uncertain, and worrying about it had Ben awake a good part of the night. In the morning, Ben and Valerie got up and headed for their car, which they had left in an empty lot down the street from their small hotel for the simple reason that he didn't have the money to pay parking fees. When he and Val reached the lot, they saw the car resting comfortably on its steel rims. During the night, somebody had jacked up the unprotected automobile and stolen the four tires.

"I felt as if I were getting sick when I saw it," Ben says. "It was the last straw. Here I was worrying myself nuts about this tournament and trying to win money—anything, even a few bucks—and I see my car without any tires. I thought for sure that it was the end. I didn't have a bit of hope left. I just felt sick. 'That's all. I can't even make it to the golf course now,' I said out loud. More than anything else in the world, I wanted to get back to Fort Worth and get some sort of a steady job. I was a complete flop and I knew it. And when you have a girl—your wife—with you and you feel like that, so helpless, it's enough to make a man go off a bridge."

At this point, Valerie took charge. She saw what a dead end Ben had reached and what was needed. She did the right thing.

"Don't be silly," she told him. "Things will be okay. We'll just ride out to the club with somebody else. Don't get upset about it."

Ben played his heart out. With his wife holding all their money—less than a dollar—Ben finished the fourth round with a very respectable 280, good for a tie for sixth place. But, more important, he won $380. No one will ever know what went on between them when Ben walked back to a waiting Valerie and told her he had placed in the money. Today, they still can't adequately describe their feelings. Hollywood did its best to make it a tear-jerking scene in the movie of Ben's life, "Follow the Sun," but it was just flat narrative compared to their real emotions that day.

When Ben speaks of those early days he just says, "They were real rough," and lets it go at that. When you examine his record and count the number of money finishes, you begin to wonder not about the faults in his putting game or the development of his driving style, but about how Ben managed to live through those lean years. The answer is an intangible one—faith. Here is a man who had more faith in what he could do with a golf stick than most people have in the future of the world.

I know from personal experience what it took to stick it out during the 1930s. You can be sure that the financial problem was a pretty serious thing for me too. Those money wins at Sacramento and Agua Caliente helped a lot to keep me in the game. Ben's win at Oakland did the same for him. Those seemingly insignificant victories prevented both of us from turning our backs on a whole way of life.

The Oakland money was enough to keep Hogan on the tournament trail, but his problems were far from being solved. He couldn't play steady enough golf to earn any of the prize money in the remaining tournaments, the Hershey

Open, the Miami-Biltmore Open, and others. It looked as if the Hogans were to face tough sledding once again. But Ben has always been a fighter, the stubborn kind who make their own breaks. One of these breaks came when he played at Hershey, Pennsylvania, where Henry Picard was the pro. Picard, although completely unaware of it himself, played an essential role in guiding Ben Hogan to the heights of golf fame.

CHAPTER 4

THE TWO COMEBACKS

When I began this immortal golf opus, I told myself, "James, keep the corn out. There's a flood of it on the market right now." In too much of my reading I've found that behind every great man there is both a woman and a Horatio Alger story. The bigger the man, the bigger the obstacles he was forced to overcome. And if he had none to climb over, you can be sure that his press agent saw to it that a few were inserted into the official biography. A political candidate, no matter how many silver spoons, forks, and knives were in his mouth at birth, simply *must* be pictured as an ex-barefoot boy who walked 10 miles daily to and from school. And the unsuspecting reader is led to believe that top entertainers always started out as movie ushers or carhops and every name athlete suffered a terrible injury which nearly ended his career before it ever started.

For professional golfers to get even mildly interested in this type of story is distinctly a novelty. We're a pretty cool lot, accustomed to hard-luck stories, dramatic comebacks, losing and winning big money on the eighteenth green. But with the story of Ben Hogan, it is different. As I think back over his career and look at the simple, cold facts, I come away with the feeling that, no matter how close I've been to golf and its trials, Hogan's life is a ready-made movie script with more natural schmaltz than even the cleverest writers and publicity men could conceive. Ben's life not only carries all the Horatio Alger ingredients but also a terrifying accident story familiar to golf lovers all over the world. It includes, as well, two genuine comebacks. One of them came after his near-fatal automobile crash. Hogan staggered out of a hospital bed and, over a period of painful months, successfully blasted his way out of the physical rough. He went back on the tournament trail, after being practically given up for dead, and played some of his greatest competitive golf.

The other comeback came following the 1937 winter tour, not long after Ben had won that dramatic $380 at Oakland. That prize money hadn't taken the Hogans very far, and tournament victories still were not coming their way. As Ben and Valerie talked it over one day at the Blackstone Hotel in Fort Worth in 1937, it seemed as if the Oakland win would be something for them to treasure for the rest of their days. Perhaps it would have to stand for all time as the biggest golf moment in the life of Ben Hogan, former professional. Completely discouraged, Ben was ready to give up the game and he was telling Valerie about it as they sat in a corner of the lobby.

Standing on the other side of the lobby that day was Henry Picard, a big money winner and a fine player, and my old friend Jack Grout. Henry glanced over at Ben and Valerie, talking quickly in the corner, and it seemed to him that they were arguing. Henry is a man with a big heart. He walked over to see if he could help out.

"What's the matter?" Henry asked.

Ben answered him quite frankly. "I don't have enough money for both of us to make the tour and I'm not going alone. Val wants me to go without her, but I won't do it. I'm giving it up."

Valerie, who had suffered plenty already at the hands of the fickle golf world, refused to let her husband give up the game even at this low point. Picard recalls that she put up a stiff argument. She knew what Ben wanted and she was going to see that he followed through. Other things could wait.

To a person of Picard's means and outlook, the matter was a simple one. Henry is a pro in more ways than one.

"All right, let's end the argument here and now. Ben, take Valerie with you and go out and play. If you need anything, come and see me. I'll take care of things."

It was just a casual-looking conversation between two men and a woman in a hotel lobby. In all it didn't take more than ten minutes. But this, according to Ben himself, was one of the moments that saved him for golf. Ben had hit the trail once, was forced to give it up, and now on his second attempt he saw the same situation developing again. This time he would quit for good; there was no hope in sight—until Picard strode across the lobby of the Blackstone Hotel that day.

"Ben and I hardly know each other, even today," Picard told me, "but he dedicated his book to me and I know that we are close friends. I'm the most surprised person in the world that what I said that day meant so much to him. And the funniest angle of all is that I never loaned Ben a penny. He never asked for it. All I did was promise to back him up. I could see he was a fine player. It would have been a shame if he left golf." Henry today is the head professional at the fine Canterbury Club in Cleveland. He admits to a "good feeling" that Hogan made the grade. "Ben has been such a credit to the game. I'm the happiest guy alive that I played even a small part in it."

From the lobby of the Blackstone, Ben headed for the Coast and there he just managed to make ends meet. He was scratching out a living with money gained from such finishes as a seventh at Los Angeles and a third-place tie at Oakland. It was still tough, but the worry and the strain seemed to decrease for him. It was heartening to have friends, especially friends who believed in you. Hogan placed third at Sacramento and fourth in the Miami Open and the money from these finishes kept him traveling, eating, and swinging. Later in the season, Picard and Ben crossed paths in the International Four-Ball matches held at the Miami Country Club. Ben, paired with Willie Goggin, lost to Picard and Johnny Revolta in the finals. Afterward, Hogan repeated the old question I'd heard before: "What do I have to do to win a match?"

For Picard—and for myself—it was not too difficult a question to answer. As I'll demonstrate later, at this stage of his career Ben was slamming the ball in low whistling drives which had a tendency to hook themselves into trouble. Picard had the answer. "Go out there and learn to slice. That's right, lift the ball and slice it. When you've found out how to do that, begin slamming it hard, with the same slicing motion. It'll straighten out and you'll be unbeatable."

I agreed entirely with Picard. It was sound advice. My own game, when it's on, always has been based on a slight fade in my shots. I knew what such advice did for me and I was confident that it would do the same for Ben. I could clearly imagine a Hogan who could fade a ball—a Hogan who could win every tournament in sight.

Before Ben changed his style and began fading his shots, he teamed with Vic Ghezzi at Hershey and won his first major tournament prior to that big year of 1940 when he really arrived. As Ghezzi and Hogan neared victory on the back nine at Hershey, you could see the desperate determination in Ben's face. Tight-lipped and grim, he played the Hershey course for all he had. "If we had lost I am quite certain that he would have jumped out of a window," Ghezzi recalls. Hershey played another important role in the Hogan story at the end of that 1939 tour. The city's pro—again, one Henry Picard—decided to accept an offer from Cleveland's Canterbury Club and gave the Hershey board of directors notice. "They asked me to help them find a successor, and they were looking at Sam Snead," Picard recalls. "But I advised them that Hogan would be the man and they listened to me."

Ben jumped at the opportunity and, for the first time in his career, he had a solid spot from which he could work. He received a respectable salary; he and Valerie ate three square meals a day; and he had a fine eighteen-hole course to practice on. By now, Ben was taking that "fade the ball" advice with him to Misery Hill (that's our name for the

The author happily displays the club and ball which gave him a hole-in-one and a low of 64 in the first day of the Ben Hogan Open in Phoenix in January of 1950 (*Acme Photo*).

The author in typical costume —red-checked cap and red-striped trousers—competing in the Los Angeles Open in 1947 (*Acme Photo*).

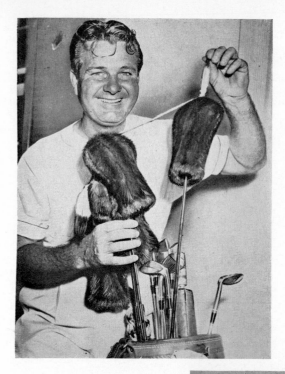

Golfers get more than their share of laughs. The author proudly displays his mink mittens for his woods (*Wide World Photos*).

The author finds a rabbit in the eighteenth hole at the Masters Tournament at Augusta in 1950 (*Wide World Photos*).

practice tee) and his game was improving daily. I remember so well watching him hit practice shots in Miami in March of 1940. I was staying with him at the Miami-Biltmore Hotel. The day we left for Augusta and the Masters, I ran into Joe Williams and Frank Graham, two fine sports writers covering major-league spring training in Florida, and they quizzed me on the golfing scene. Mostly they asked questions about my own game and chances of success in the coming tournaments. But all the while I felt they were missing the important story and finally I told them so.

"What's that?" Graham asked.

"Ben Hogan's new game," I answered.

The next time the world heard from Hogan was a few weeks later at Pinehurst, North Carolina, where the North and South Open was held. With his new fading drive and a sharper putting game, he slammed the ball around with such force and accuracy that he earned his first major individual victory with a score of 277—a record for the event which still stands today.

That Pinehurst victory spelled out the arrival of Ben Hogan, unbeatable golfer. I remember that North and South clearly and my thoughts on the occasion. "I don't think," I said to a friend after it was over, "that there are many golfers who are going to be able to beat Hogan from now on. He is just about ready to take charge. The worryin' days are over—for Ben. And they're just starting for the rest of us!" This marked the end of those "When am I ever going to win?" questions that Ben would put quietly to his close friends. If he ever asked the question again, I would have a ready answer. "Tomorrow."

Once on the winning trail, he was there for good. After the North and South victory, he captured the Greensboro Open, then the Asheville "Land in the Sky" Open and the Goodall Round Robin. He was second in the Chicago Open and fourth at Milwaukee. Shooting winning golf in every tournament, he wound up the year with $10,656 in prizes, making him the year's top money winner. In 1941 he picked up even more momentum. He teamed with veteran Gene Sarazen to capture the Miami Four-Ball, he took a third in the Open, and then won the Asheville, Chicago, and Hershey Tournaments. It was also in 1941 that Ben and I collaborated on one of our Inverness Four-Ball triumphs. In 39 tournaments, *he finished lower than fifth only once,* and came away from the tour with $18,358 in winnings. At this point, he had established himself as *the* golfer. At the end of the '41 season, he had been in the money through 56 straight tournaments, a record which still stands. The outlook for his opponents was strictly bleak.

In 1942, Ben was the leading money winner again, earning $13,143 in prizes, but his immediate future was being decided by a few people personally unacquainted with Hogan in Berlin and Tokyo. Just as it appeared that Ben was to reach the golfing heights for which he had worked so hard for so many years, he was called away from golf and into the service.

I was home in Houston when the Japanese worked over Pearl Harbor. The Navy gave me a job without too much hesitation and the new clothes style for Demaret consisted of wide-bottomed trousers and a somewhat drab blue shirt. Ben went into the Army Air Corps and both of us put in a few frustrating years—as did a few million other Americans.

For Hogan, the news that Byron Nelson was ruling golf with an iron hand—Byron won $37,967 in 1944 and $63,335 in 1944, all in War Bonds—was an added bit of frustration. Byron was unable to serve his nation because of a dangerous case of hemophilia. For Ben, the thought that somebody else was on top of the golf heap was a galling one, even when that person was his old friend Byron Nelson. In my opinion Byron is one of the four greatest golfers of all time, and even today he leaves his Texas farm every now and then to compete in some tournament and flashes as fine a game of golf as there is in the business. But Ben, a proud and fierce competitor, just couldn't sit still with the thought that somebody—anybody—was ruling the golf world when he wasn't around to contest it.

He got his chance just after the war in the latter part of 1945 and early in 1946. His game was as good as ever. He came through with five tournament victories, including a Professional Golfers' Association scoring record of 261 for the 72-hole Portland, Oregon, invitational tournament. He won by 17 strokes over Nelson and finished an unbelievable 27 under par. After the tournament, I congratulated Hogan with an innocuous "Nice going, Ben" or some such remark. He answered with a tight smile. "I guess that takes care of this 'Mr. Golf' business." He was referring to the title given Nelson during the war by the newspaper boys.

In 1946, Ben continued to make up for lost time by racking up an unprecedented 13 consecutive triumphs to begin the year—two of them four-ball events with myself. Once again he was the leading money winner, this time with

$42,556. In 1947, it was nearly the same story, with Hogan becoming more and more impossible to beat. But one victory kept eluding him—the U.S. Open. He was fourth in 1946 (Mangrum beat Ghezzi and Nelson in a playoff) and sixth the next year when Lew Worsham won it. The Open is the big one for American golfers. It carries with it a special prestige that no other tournament can boast. Although not the richest, it is still the World Series of golf. But why Hogan had to pick 1948 as his first year to win the Open is something I shall never know. It was held at the Riviera Country Club at Los Angeles, and afterward a Los Angeles newspaper renamed the course "Hogan's Alley." Ben toured the course for a winning 72-hole total of 276, five strokes under the record set by Ralph Guldahl in 1937. It was also two strokes under the record which had been set earlier that same day by one Jimmy Demaret. But why dwell on such memories? Someone has to lose.

Since that day, Ben has won three other U.S. Opens, and I believe he is planning on three or four more. Some of our statisticians and record keepers claim that Hogan has already won five U.S. Opens, rather than four. They maintain that the Hale America Tournament in 1942, which Ben won with a four-round total of 271, was actually the Open in wartime disguise and that the victor received the same medal awarded to winners of the U.S. Open. But let's allow those nearsighted students of record books to stew over that one.

The next time Ben Hogan was forced to make a comeback it was of a very different nature. After a terrible—and that's the only word for it—automobile accident, he pulled together a broken and pain-racked body, learned to walk and move about again, hit another million balls off the practice tee, gradually regained his strength and skill, and started a second, even greater, golfing career. They have to pull out all the stops and run down a long list of adjectives to describe this one—stirring . . . unbelievable . . . great . . . magnificent. The newspaper boys called it everything they could think of and in bold type. But I have a different feeling about Ben and the accident. Perhaps that's only natural since I was pretty close to it.

The story—which to me will always be a near-tragedy more than a glorious comeback—began in the Long Beach Open in January of 1949. Ben and I tied for first place in that tournament, and in a playoff, my pardner Ben made off with the $2,000 first prize as usual. After that, we went to Phoenix and again a Demaret-Hogan tie developed for top money, in the Arizona city's Open. This time I managed to keep my drives a bit straighter down the fairways of the Phoenix Country Club course and came away with that rare thing, a victory over Ben in a playoff, as well as the winner's share of $1,400. We were sitting around over drinks after the playoff and I asked Ben if he was coming along to Tucson to see if we could cook up a rubber match.

"No, Val and I want to get back to Fort Worth," he answered. "No sense having a house if we don't live in it." The Hogans had bought a house only eight days before leaving on the tour, and, like all new homeowners, they were anxious to get back so that Valerie could bring her woman's eye to bear on the interior furnishings. It was 1949 and things were going smoothly for Ben. Since he was winning more than his share of the big tournaments, he didn't feel pushed to compete in all of them.

"What's the matter? I beat you in one playoff and you have to run home and practice for a month?" That was my parting remark to Ben as I left for Tucson and he and Valerie climbed into their beautiful new Cadillac and headed for home. We had a laugh over it. Later I had cause to remember my little joke with mixed feelings.

On Wednesday, February 2, a heavy fog clung to United States Highway 80, which runs across the dusty plains of West Texas. Ben and Valerie were 200 miles outside of El Paso at a tiny place called Van Horne, and he was carefully picking his way through the fog at 10 miles an hour. It was hard to see anything other than the few feet of concrete road directly in front of the car, but Ben did make out the two headlights of an oncoming truck in the opposite lane. Those two headlights suddenly became four as a ten-ton Greyhound bus swerved out to pass the truck and roared directly at the Hogans. It was only a two-lane highway and off the road to Ben's right was a deep culvert.

The big bus rolled forward at a high speed, the driver never appearing to see the Hogans' car. Ben didn't have a chance to avoid the head-on collision. At the last moment, he let go of the wheel and threw his body in front of Valerie just as the bus smashed into them. As it turned out, that move saved his life and probably hers. With the crunch of ripping metal and the screeching of brakes, the bus and car collided, and the steering wheel of Ben's car whistled straight back and buried itself in the seat. If Hogan had stayed behind the wheel and had not tried to protect his wife, he would have been impaled on the steering apparatus and undoubtedly killed. The truck swerved off the highway and another car ran into it. A fifth vehicle, blinded by the fog, slammed into the tangled mass of truck, bus, and cars before emergency signals could be set up and traffic halted.

Valerie Hogan came out of a fuzzy state of semiconsciousness with Ben's head in her lap. She herself was only bruised, but her husband lay motionless on the ground. He didn't even appear to be breathing. From the little knot of people surrounding them, a voice said, "He's dead." Then somebody else came over and put a blanket over his body. As they attempted to cover Ben's face, Valerie snatched the blanket off.

Shocked and frightened to the point of hysteria, Valerie simply sat by her husband's lifeless form. Somebody knelt at her side and tried to give Ben first aid. "Where's that ambulance?" another said. People moved away to see if aid was coming. Then Ben stirred—just moved and groaned a little. But it was enough to let Valerie know he was alive. She looked hopefully for some sign of an ambulance or a doctor who could help her husband. An hour and a half later, Valerie was still looking. In the confusion and worry which followed the accident, nobody made a move to get help. It was one of those terrible situations where people just assume help is going to materialize, or that somebody else has taken the necessary steps. Finally, somebody had the sense to summon aid and an ambulance arrived. As it left, lights winking and siren wailing, I'm told that someone began to gather up Ben's clubs which were sprayed across the road. Certainly no one at the scene of the accident that night ever dreamed he would use them again.

The ambulance carried Ben's shocked and shattered body 119 miles to the Hotel Dieu, a hospital at El Paso. His pelvis was fractured, as were his left collarbone, left ankle, and several ribs. It was four hours after the accident that Ben was carried into the hospital. At first glance, the doctors there gave him only a slim chance to survive.

As this tragedy was taking place, I was walking over the sun-splashed Tucson golf course, playing in the pro-amateur event with Del Webb, the owner of the New York Yankees, Hi Corbett, Tucson sportsman, and Tony Penna, the New York City pro. We were working our way down the sixth hole, when the Tucson Country Club manager came running across the fairway and hailed us.

"I just heard on the radio that Ben Hogan was killed in an auto crash this morning," he called.

For what seemed like an hour he didn't get an answer. The others knew Ben, although not as well as I, and that one sentence hit each of us squarely and viciously in the solar plexus. I don't remember what I said exactly, but I began walking to the clubhouse. I wanted to get at a phone. I remember Webb softly calling to the caddies and paying them off. I even recall his exact words. "I think we'll forget about golf for today."

At the clubhouse, I called the Texas State Highway Department and asked them if they had any report on Ben Hogan being killed in an auto accident. The man on the other end said he'd check and call me back. I hung up and stood there looking dumbly at the wall in front of me. Then the fellow called me back. "Yes," he said, "Hogan was in an accident. But he's alive. He's at the Hotel Dieu in El Paso."

It felt good, damned good, just to know that he was alive. I called the hospital and was told that Ben was on the critical list, but when I pressed them for some more information, a doctor came on and said that Ben looked as if he would recover.

For two days he couldn't be moved, and it was during this time that the iron body Ben had built up over years on the tournament trail squared off with—and beat—that old man with the scythe. Ben overcame shock and his broken body kept on functioning. On his third day in the hospital, Friday, they took X rays and encased his body in a plaster cast from his chest to his knees and another on his ankle. He was in this condition when I arrived on Monday, after driving over from Tucson. All the way up to his room I was trying to think what to say to him. You know, one of those sunny "get well" remarks, but the words weren't forming. When I walked into his room, I just gave him a natural greeting, natural for us anyway.

"Ben, you old sonofabitch. Just because I beat you in a playoff, you didn't have to get so mad that you tried to run a bus off the road."

The little man got a kick out of it. He gave a weak laugh and then said, "Aw, I'll beat this thing." A little later he said it again. "I'll be back there playing real soon." But the doctors made no secret of their opinion. He was never going to be able to play golf again, they had told me. It made it difficult to look at Ben and say, "Sure, you'll be out there in another playoff with me before you know it."

After a week had gone by, it seemed that the little man's optimism might be at least partially justified. He made satisfactory progress and after another examination he was told that he could make the trip home to Forth Worth in a few days. But on February 18, Ben lost a round in his battle with those innumerable injuries. A blood clot moved up from Ben's left leg and reached his lungs. His condition took a downward spiral, and a week later another clot moved to the same spot. Now the talk was of saving Hogan's life instead of traveling to Fort Worth.

His weight dropped from a normal 142 to a weak 115 pounds. Teams of doctors used every drug and technique in the books in the fight to save Hogan's life. One of the drugs apparently had a bad effect on him, causing bleeding. The doctors at the Hotel Dieu urged an operation in which the vena cava, the vein which drains the pelvis and both legs, would be tied off to prevent any more movement of clots from that area. After a conference with Valerie and (by phone) with doctors at the Mayo Clinic in Rochester, Minnesota, the Texas hospital recommended Dr. Alton S. Ochsner, professor of surgery at Tulane University in New Orleans.

Valerie called Dr. Ochsner. He was ready and willing to come immediately, but commercial service had been tied up between Fort Worth and New Orleans by a rainstorm. There were no chartered planes available. While these transportation problems were being talked out, Ben was slowly slipping. He became delirious. During that long night, he began calling for caddies to give him clubs and for galleries to move back while he shot. Somebody had to dig up an airplane and in a hurry. Royal Hogan, Ben's brother, got on the telephone and called Brig. Gen. David W. Hutchinson, commanding officer at the Briggs Air Force Base at El Paso. Ben and General Hutchinson were friends, and Royal asked for a favor. By morning, a B-29 had landed Dr. Ochsner in El Paso and the doctor advised an immediate operation.

Valerie, however, wouldn't make the decision unless Ben gave his okay. When Ben regained consciousness, the doctor came in and explained just what he would do in the operation. He pointed out to Ben how the tied-off vena cava would force the blood to return to his heart through many other channels. Ben listened, but he only wanted to know one thing: "Are you going to fix me so that I can play golf again?"

In truth, Dr. Ochsner thought Ben would be a lucky man if he ever walked properly again, much less competed in golf tournaments. But he told Ben that he thought his playing golf again a possibility. And I don't think the doctor was telling a lie, either. Nothing is impossible—especially when you are dealing with a man of such proven courage and spirit.

With Hogan's consent the cast was removed from his body and Dr. Ochsner began the delicate operation. Valerie, exhausted from the strain and tension, went into the hospital chapel and prayed during most of the two-hour operation. Dr. Ochsner did his work well, and it was thought that the operation saved Ben's life—but at the price of his golf career. His left leg was a battered and scarred appendage, with vital circulation slowed to an absolute minimum.

It was at this point, I would say, that Ben hit the golf comeback trail a second time. He began the long task of getting himself ready for golf again almost the minute he came out from under the ether. I visited him at the hospital a few days after the operation and I almost had to laugh at the sight of my man. He had developed a little "Misery Hill" of his own right on the bed. When I walked into the room, the first thing I saw was Ben fondling his putter. Sitting there in bed, propped up by pillows, he waggled the stick around in the air and practiced gripping it. I would like to bet that he asked for the golf club before he asked for a drink of water.

Then I took a close look at the bed itself. Hanging over it was one of those gymnasium-type bars, the kind of gadget suspended from the ceiling that I used to call a monkey swing. Ben's left collarbone had not yet mended and he couldn't use that arm, but with his good right hand he was grabbing that bar and lifting himself up in a series of daily exercises. On the table next to the bed were two small rubber balls. Already he was using them for squeezing exercises to strengthen his hands.

"You've got yourself a regular little training camp here, Hawk," I told him. I don't know what the doctors were saying about his condition at that time. As for me, I went away from the hospital that day with a big smile on my face, absolutely certain that Ben was going to play golf again. In fact I had the fleeting suspicion that he would come back stronger than a gorilla with all that gymnasium work he was putting in.

While he was in bed at the Hotel Dieu, something else was happening to Ben. He watched unbelievingly as a flood of mail and telegrams was placed in his room every morning. He heard of the hundreds of phone calls which swamped the switchboard. Valerie began reading off the names of people who had sent him the wires and letters. "I don't even know that name," Ben would say time and again, with a puzzled look on his face.

Then, perhaps for the first time in his life, he began to understand a few things about the American sporting public, things he had overlooked as he mercilessly whipped himself to the top of his profession. "I never realized how swell the American people can be," he said. And the little pleasures he had never had the time to care about began to become important. "You can't imagine," he said, "how wonderful it is just to be able to sit and talk with people." His brush with death had made him appreciate that there were other things in life besides a golf club and a four-under-par 68. He never got over the letters and wires from people he'd never met, people he probably never would meet. The country's honest concern for his welfare, *off the golf course as well as on it,* changed his entire outlook.

You can see it in Hogan today. Instead of the tight-lipped man who so closely resembled an old-time wild West frontier sheriff, Ben is a more relaxed and outward-going fellow. He knows how to take it easy. He enjoys meeting people. He's learned how nice just being alive can be.

Exactly twelve days after the operation, Ben was able to get out of his hospital bed unaided. It was the first time in over six weeks that he had put both feet on the floor and, as far as he was concerned, it was the appropriate moment to begin mapping his comeback strategy. Several weeks later, he pulled himself onto a Pullman car, a gaunt but smiling figure, for the ride home to Fort Worth. At the station in Fort Worth, an ambulance picked him up and took him to his house. Back home, he would start off nearly every conversation with "When I play golf again . . . ," and Valerie would smile. Doctor after doctor had told her that Ben was never going to be able to play golf again. But these were only doctors. They didn't know her husband. He said he was going to play again and she believed him.

Ben planned his recovery with scientific detachment. He was going to handle the situation "just like a round of golf. I'm going to play it one shot at a time." So Ben began the long, painful grind with one of those "walkers" they give recuperating patients, a device which you move by paddling with your feet, like a kiddie car. That Hogan mania for practice—plus Valerie's gentle support—went into his walker, and after a while Ben was able to move around on the apparatus pretty well. For three weeks he practiced in it, and then he was ready to solo. The next step was taken, literally, when he began limping laps around his living room. He did it progressively. First he painfully made his way around the living room, unaided, five times. Then he'd come back and do it ten times. Then fifteen. The living room rug began to take a fearful beating.

Next on the agenda was a walk around the block. Just a simple walk around the block. But it took Ben days to accomplish it. At first, he couldn't make it even around the house. Then he'd have to sit on the curb before he had finished even half of his projected stroll, and wait for Valerie to pick him up in the car. But he was practicing. Pretty soon people who lived a mile or so away could look out their window and see Ben Hogan walking by. Then, a few weeks later, they would see him jogging a few steps. He was on his way back now. We all knew it.

With the problem of walking apparently solved, Ben began to think of golf. He sat down in May and wrote a letter to the United States Golf Association, and it was a bit of a bombshell when it reached that group's headquarters in New York City. "Enclosed," it said, "is my entry for the Open with the hope that I'll be able to play. Up to now, I haven't taken a swing. But miracles may happen. Would you please do me a favor and not release my entry to the press? If I can play, I should like it to be a surprise. I hope and pray that I may play in June."

But he had been too optimistic. By June, Ben was still trying to walk and move about naturally, and golf was out of the question. His "surprise" request in the letter to the U.S.G.A., however, always makes me smile a bit. If you know golf and realize how much old Sam Snead worries about Ben Hogan, you can easily envision the look which would have settled on the country gentleman's face if Ben had appeared for that Open.

In August, Hogan made two trips to New Orleans for examinations by Dr. Ochsner and on the second one, the surgeon noted that the cartilage in his right knee was torn. An operation was advised, but Hogan had reached the end as far as hospitals and operations were concerned. He'd have none of it. I stopped in to see Ben during that month and told him the professionals wanted him to be the nonplaying captain of the Ryder Cup team which was to meet England's best in September overseas. Ben came along with us and, as

I have described, turned himself into the toughest captain I've ever heard of. "Hey, Hawk! We training for golf or for the Army?" I asked him more than once on that trip.

All Ben was able to do in England was to watch and force his team to get in a little practice time. But when he came back to Fort Worth, he picked up those golf sticks and began practicing. He dragged himself out to the Colonial Country Club and started to hit golf balls. At first, he must have been a pathetic figure. He could move his legs very little. He hit the ball from a still position with his arms. His caddy that first day remarked that "he looked all right when he putted and chipped, but when he tried to hit some wood shots I couldn't believe this was Ben Hogan. A little kid could have hit a longer ball."

Golf writers around the nation were almost unanimous in thinking that Hogan would not play again. "He'll never play again," they were telling the nation. "If he does, he'll be lucky to break 90. America has lost a great athlete." But while people were mourning the end of his career, Ben was down there at Fort Worth hitting golf balls by the thousands —and talking himself and others into the belief that he'd play again. "Look at Craig Wood. He won the Open in 1941 with a taped-up back," Ben would say. "Or take Ed Furgol. His left arm is shriveled, but he still plays a terrific game. Listen, a lot of people have had bad injuries. They came back and so will I."

Bill Rives, the sports editor of the *Dallas News*, was one who came away with the feeling that golf would see more of Ben. "You can't write off Ben Hogan. You can't count ten over him until he's had his chance," Rives wrote in August after a talk with Ben. "I spoke to him and came away with the feeling that he had a fine chance to make it. He was so confident." Rives brought up the question of age, but Hogan "even had an answer for that. 'You're thirty-seven now,' I told him. 'Supposing it takes until you are forty before you can play again. What about that?'"

"Age makes no difference," Hogan answered. "If a man has the desire, he can play. The trouble with most men is that they lose the desire after they get around forty years old. They'd rather sit in the clubhouse than get out and practice." The Hawk was being very objective and practical about his resumption of tournament golf. He knew his injuries would force him to change his swing and his stance somewhat. "I guess I'll have to let a little of my distance go in order to control the ball better," he explained.

By January of 1950, only a year after the accident, Ben Hogan was up and ready. He was on the practice tee at the Riviera Club at Los Angeles, getting warmed up for the Los Angeles Open. I was with Lloyd Mangrum and Jackie Burke when Ben checked in for the tournament. When he headed, inevitably, toward that practice tee, we went down to watch him. I had an inkling of what we were going to see. Lloyd and Jackie had been reading the newspaper accounts of his injuries and had adopted their pessimistic tone about a comeback. I was convinced of the opposite. I was sure Ben wasn't entering any tournament unless he was in top shape and had a chance to win.

When we reached the tee, there was no question about it. The little man was knocking the caddy's feet out from under him with those dead-to-the-pin shots. He was getting plenty of distance and pin-point accuracy with every club in the bag. He hit seven balls and not one of them landed more than a few yards from the others. He himself still looked gaunt, but the obvious health of his golf game compensated.

All I could think of to say was, "Looks to me like you've been practicing a bit." It's hard to describe what a wonderful feeling it was to see Ben hitting the ball like that. And I wasn't kidding myself about another aspect of the situation either—his return to form was money out of my pocket.

"No, I've been out for a long time, Jimmy," Ben answered solemnly. "I'm just going to try my luck here."

His dead-pan answer didn't fool me even a little bit. "Let me get a look at those hands of yours, boy," I said, and Jackie and I grabbed one and took a long look. The hand was sporting so many calluses it might have belonged to a man who just chopped down a redwood tree. That told the story right there. To be able to swing a golf club properly over a long tournament, your hands have to be tough. The only way to harden them is by long hours of practice. And Ben's hands were tough as shoeleather.

"Why, you could reface your driver with the palm of your hand instead of using a wood rasp," I told him. We laughed and shook hands with the man who had returned. It was like putting your hand into a meat grinder just to shake with him.

He was ready for the tournament, I found out later, because of a few little items like an eighteen-hole stint as early as the day after Christmas. Ben had used a motor scooter to get around the course that first time but soon he was able to do without it. If any doubts remained in our minds about the completeness of his recovery, that first practice round in Los Angeles dispelled them. We played together and it was the first golf I'd seen Ben shoot since I beat him in that Phoenix playoff a year before. Yet it seemed as if he hadn't been away from golf for more than eight hours. He walked over that course and absolutely wrecked par, coming home with a 68. His woods were perhaps not quite as long as before, but plenty long enough. His irons were operating like Detroit-made machines, and his putter was behaving nicely. Ben Hogan was once again the man to beat.

It must have been a heartwarming occasion for Ben when he stepped onto the tee for his first shot in the tournament itself. He had requested the announcer, Scotty Chisholm, to introduce him simply. Scotty, in his kilts and tam, followed Ben's wishes. "This is the greatest event in the history of the Los Angeles Open," he said. "But I have been requested by Mr. Hogan to introduce him and say nothing else. On the tee is Ben Hogan!" The gallery let out a roar. It seemed to embarrass The Hawk. He walked up to the tee and then turned around and looked at the people yelling for him. Once again, Ben was finding out that he had a lot of unknown friends who cared about him. They continued to yell and he sort of bowed his head a little.

Then he turned around and played golf. He shot a respectable round of 73 to keep him in the running, but at the end of his first day of competitive golf he had to drag himself back to bed. He was finding out just how much that accident had taken out of him. Despite all his hard work and the many practice rounds, Ben found walking a painful chore under actual tournament pressure. His legs began to drag, his back ached, each step felt as if it should have been the last.

The next day out, Ben shot a 69—and it began to rain. The dampness seeped into his still-healing joints and he must have been in considerable pain. Yet you would have assumed him to be in top shape from his scores. He followed his second-round 69 with two more of the same for a four-round total of 280, which is pretty fine golf from any viewpoint. It looked good enough to win the tournament, but while Ben was resting in his room at the club, old Sam Snead was coming home with a remarkable 66 and a 20-foot putt to tie Ben and force a playoff.

"I wish he had won today," Ben said when informed of the playoff. Dead tired though he was, I know that Hogan was a very happy man. He had shown he could play winning golf again. What happened in the playoff was strictly anticlimatic. Sam bettered Hogan's 76 by several strokes to win easily. But I don't think anybody who saw that tournament had any doubt left that Hogan was back to stay. As Snead walked off the winner on the eighteenth green, Grantland Rice, the dean of sports writers, made a remark which I'll remember for the rest of my life. "His legs weren't strong enough to carry his heart around," Granny said as he watched Hogan head for the clubhouse. That about summed it up.

Two months later, Ben appeared at the Augusta National course for the Masters, a tournament which he never had won. I put together a few hot rounds and won that event with a 281, and Ben finished in a tie for fourth place with a 288. Some loose tongues started to wag a bit after that tournament. A few stupid people claimed, in whispers, that Ben was able to play good enough golf, all right, but it appeared to them that the grand old unbeatable Hogan was no more. Then some yarns about his being completely through popped up again. When I heard them, I wanted to bust out laughing. Here the man gets out of a hospital bed, shakes off a few broken limbs, takes a first-place tie in one tournament and a fourth in another, and people claim he ain't what he used to be. It was ridiculous.

Three weeks later Ben went out and tore the Greenbrier course apart at the seams as he won the White Sulphur Springs event with a 259, the lowest score ever shot in American competition. Then everybody realized just how ridiculous those rumors were.

We were beginning to realize something else, too, as Ben took a third in the Colonial Club event at Fort Worth and then finished well up in the Celebrities Tournament at Washington, D.C. Once again he was aiming squarely for the U.S. Open championship to be held over the rugged Merion course at Haverford, Pennsylvania.

Such was the case. The 1950 Open became his comeback goal. He started out with a 72 on that first day, Thursday, and then brought his score down, characteristically, to a 69 on Friday. Now he faced Saturday's thirty-six-hole grind. With his game well under control he shot a 72 in the morning, leaving himself two strokes off the pace. That, we have learned over the years, is the best Hogan spot. Most of the pressure, a lot of which he generates himself, is on the leaders. They know, and Ben knows, that The Hawk is going to be awfully tough in that final eighteen. In that last round, it seemed everybody faded but Hogan, who only needed pars on the last five holes to win. This was the tournament, previously described, in which Ben blew up on the seventeenth and then showed that tremendous nerve of his by coming in with a birdie to tie on the last hole. The next day he ran away from Mangrum and George Fazio in the playoff and took the crown.

From that point on, Hogan really went to work building up the legend. I won't bore you (and annoy myself) with a complete list of his victories. The Masters, the tournament he'd never won, fell to him in 1951. Then the cruelly rigged Oakland Hills course in Detroit faded under his "greatest round" and the little man had his third Open championship in succession. As he piled up victory after victory, his once thin body filled out to a husky 170 pounds of pure golf champion.

As a footnote to the accident story, I might mention that the bus company settled with Ben for an ample sum of money —rumored to be something between $125,000 and a half million. Shortly after the settlement I buttonholed The Hawk in a Los Angeles hotel and ribbed him about owning a piece of that bus company. It was being whispered about the golf world, I said, that every morning he called the dispatcher in Fort Worth to see that his busses were running on schedule.

But no matter how obvious the gag, the little man always pulls a long face. "Jimmy, don't say a thing like that!" He looked around for eavesdroppers. "People will think I've got money. They'll hound me!"

That's the story of Ben Hogan's two comebacks. Twice he

was down, once in spirit and the second time physically flat on his back. Each time he stepped back into the pit and asked no quarter. Very seldom did he mention his accident injuries before or during a tournament. There were no alibis if he lost. Usually the only emotion he registers in defeat is surprise. You see, he thought he was going to win.

CHAPTER 5

A PROFILE OF THE MAN

Right here, I'd like to introduce you to a friend of mine. He's not an easy boy to know, but friendship with Ben is definitely worth the effort. He is a man of strong character and fine qualities. He is difficult to know for a couple of simple reasons. One is that he is an introvert, plain and simple. The other is that he spends most of his time out on a golf course. If you've been reading about Ben Hogan over the years, you've probably seen a lot of negative reports about his relations with people. Some have described him as cold. I once read that he would make "the perfect gun-toting, tight-lipped Texan if these were still the frontier days." Others have noted his early differences with the press. Still others have said that he is nothing more than a golfing machine. Perhaps elements of these reports have truth in them. Certainly on the golf course, Hogan is a grim-faced, tight-lipped automaton. But take it from someone who knows him well—he is also a fine, courageous, and warmhearted human being.

In trying to describe Ben Hogan the man, I am dealing with two very different personalities. The Ben Hogan who toured the country before his accident is a lot different from the man we know today. A brush with death, in my opinion, changed his outlook in many ways. There are, however, two notable exceptions to that statement. Hogan is a man of impeccable integrity and he always has been—accident or no accident. And through the years, I have never met a man more seriously dedicated to his mission in golf.

People in golf feel that Ben invented the word honesty. In all his dealings, both on and off a golf course, Hogan does everything strictly according to the truth of the matter. For instance, just before that 1950 U.S. Open playoff between George Fazio, Lloyd Mangrum, and Hogan that I mentioned before, Ben was approached by Ed Sullivan, a syndicated columnist and television impresario, who guaranteed him a thousand dollars to appear after the playoff on his "Toast of the Town" TV program whether Ben won or lost. Ben agreed to appear.

He won the playoff handily and immediately afterward was offered $1,500 to perform on another show. A lesser man might have consented to appear on both shows (Sullivan had no exclusive contract at this point) or might simply have accepted the higher offer. Such alternatives never crossed Ben's mind. Sullivan had made his guarantee *before* the Open playoff, win, lose, or draw. The more attractive offer went begging.

Ben sticks to an honest bargain and constantly honors

the truth until it hurts—and it certainly wasn't painless that time. On another occasion, his absolute honesty cost him what might have amounted to a fat sum of money. Bob Brumby, the golf writer, had come up with a solid idea for a business venture and he went to Ben with it. They were driving between Phoenix and Tucson one day when Brumby made the proposal.

"Ben," Brumby said, "how would you like to start a chain of golf schools all across the country—the same thing Arthur Murray has done with his dance studios. We'd call it 'The Ben Hogan School of Golf.' We could hire professionals for each school, train them in your technique, and then find space in a big department store in every large city in the country."

Ben listened carefully. "It sounds good," he said finally. "But it's impossible, Bob. It would require too much of my time. I wouldn't be able to do anything but teach in those schools. And I don't know about all the money. I'd only be able to teach in one at a time open."

"It wouldn't take much time," Brumby answered. "All you'd have to do is train the pros for a month or so and then take a tour of your schools maybe once a year. You'd have all the time in the world to play."

Hogan turned to the writer in surprise. "Oh, no! I couldn't let people pay for a golf lesson under my name unless I was there to give it myself. I couldn't ask anybody to take a Ben Hogan lesson unless I was the teacher."

"When Ben said that, I saw about a half million dollars

going out the car window," Brumby told me. "But, you know, I didn't even mind. I felt good. I was with a man who was honest right down to the core."

On the circuit, Ben refuses to join any of the card games his fellow pros indulge in at almost every club they hit. He feels he should concentrate only on golf while on the circuit and that evenings should be for sleep and thinking about the next day's play. But there's little doubt that he can make those cards do tricks. I remember back in 1946, after Ben had won the San Francisco Match Play Tournament, Holly Goodrich and Bob Hudson, two sportsmen from Portland, got together with Ben and me for a little chat and smoke session in the country-club grill. Along about eleven that evening, Hudson wanted to play some cards and I asked Ben to show us a few tricks. He was relaxed and enjoying the company a lot and for once he consented to pick up a deck of cards and show the people what he could make them do. He began dealing the cards around, flicking them out so quickly you couldn't tell how many you had or where they came from. Then he sat back and named every card in our hands. He went so far as to tell us he'd once dealt a good many hands of faro. That night he could have made the best night club magician look like an amateur. I half expected to see him take a pink handkerchief out of his cuff and make a parachute out of it.

Hogan is a man of his word. He is absolutely dependable. I have never known him to give a promise and then not produce. In August of 1953, right after he had returned from his British Open triumph and was at the height of his popularity, the professional at the Foresgate Country Club in Jamesburg, New Jersey, Jerre Volpe, called Hogan long distance on a sudden whim. Although he didn't know Ben personally, Volpe asked him to play in an exhibition match in Jamesburg. Much to Volpe's surprise, Hogan asked the terms, agreed to a date, and then hung up. Later in the week, when plans for the exhibition were in full swing, Volpe and the golf committee got the jitters. After all, it was only a brief phone conversation—what if he didn't show up? What if he forgot? *Everybody* wanted Hogan—why should he come to a club in New Jersey? A member of the committee telephoned me and I assured him that Hogan would appear as promised. But that wasn't enough. They persuaded two other friends of Ben's to call him long distance just to make positive. At the second call he hit the ceiling. "What do those guys want?" he yelled across the wires. "A sworn statement? Tell them I'll be there and that I'll play eighteen holes! Doesn't anybody believe me?" Needless to say he was as good as his word.

Hogan has always been a very serious fellow. With Ben, every move is important and must be carefully weighed. When he is talking about anything except an out-and-out joke, he remains absolutely dead-panned. He listens carefully to others and his opinions, when he delivers them, don't have even the hint of a light touch in them. Sometimes he goes to extremes and upsets himself unnecessarily. I had a rather gruesome example of this in 1949. Returning from England on the *Queen Elizabeth* after the Ryder Cup trip, we ran into a stormy crossing. The biggest ship in the world was rolling about like a 15-foot dinghy on our first night out. At about five in the morning, I grew tired of tossing around in bed and I took a stroll to the bar to forget about the weather. Ben was walking around the deck, painfully. He still hadn't fully recuperated from the accident and the rough voyage was bothering him a good deal.

"Come on, Hawk, I'll buy you a drink," I told him and he followed me into the bar. Ben turned down the drink and let out a few moans about the way he felt. I knew he must have been in considerable pain, because this fellow has never been a weeper. When he doesn't feel well, he usually makes a point of telling no one. While we were standing at the bar, I looked up into the mirror and through the open door I saw a crowd of seamen and a minister at the rail. It probably would have been better if we had stayed at the bar but we walked out to see what was up. They were conducting a sea burial for one of the crew. He had died during the night and, for some reason, they were not keeping the body. A big flag was draped over it and the crewmen were just pushing the body overboard. I stiffened a bit and got set to turn right around and head back to the bar. But Ben grabbed me by the arm.

"Jimmy," he said. "Please. Whatever happens to me, don't let them do that. You're my friend. Don't let them do that to me if I die on this thing."

It wasn't a joke. Ben meant every word of it. This was carrying things just a bit too far, but all I could think of was a corny crack. "Ben, don't you worry. The water here is too cold for you. If anything happens, we'll wait until the ship gets into warmer water."

He didn't crack a smile.

He carries his serious thoughts and somber moods even into his sleep at night. Bing Crosby coined another nickname for The Hawk after hearing about his sleeping habits one night at the crooner's ranch in Tuscarora, Nevada. I bunked with Ben that night and at about two in the morning a peculiar grinding noise woke me up. Now, Bing keeps a pretty clean place and it surprised me. I didn't want to believe it, but you could have had my bottom dollar that rats were scrambling all over the room. I walked down the hall and got Crosby. They were *his* rats, after all. He came back with me and listened for a moment. Then he pointed at Hogan. The noise was the steady grinding of Ben's teeth. He had a problem of some sort on his mind and he'd taken it right to bed with him. Crosby was laying for Ben when he came down to breakfast in the morning. Bing grabbed him by the jaw and forced his mouth open.

"There you are—finest blades ever honed. Old Blue Blades himself."

It was just Bing's joke until I looked at Ben's teeth. They were the shortest set of teeth I've ever seen. Obviously that wasn't his first night of worrying and grinding.

Until 1949, Ben was a feverish little guy, driving himself relentlessly from tournament to tournament with a desire to win which blotted everything else from his mind. Nothing mattered except winning a golf tournament, not even making new friends or speaking to old acquaintances. He had no time. He was too busy concentrating on his game. There were too many lean days which he wanted to make up for. But while he was doing everything right on the golf course, he was making mistakes off it—mistakes which brought him a steady stream of criticism from the newspapers.

For instance, at one tournament he did not realize he had won, this feverish pace caused him to leave right after he holed his last putt. He rushed back to the hotel, leaving the committee and its awards ceremony looking around for the winner. The newspapers set up an anguished howl and Hogan howled right back. He tried to explain the misunderstanding and his reasons for leaving right after the tournament but to no avail. On this and other occasions his critics didn't grasp the fanatical urge to win which was driving him on. He could hardly wait, even for a matter of minutes, after winning a tournament. He wanted to hop into the car with Valerie and drive to the next club. He needed more practice, he'd have to look over the course, he was late already. . . . This drive to win was overstepping its bounds—but Ben didn't realize it.

With his usual honesty, he told the writers they were all wrong. He told them so in person and he called them up from wherever he was. He'd call New York, he'd call Los Angeles, he'd call any writer—even the very biggest—and personally blast him if his writings were critical or even slightly in error. For years Ben didn't seem to realize the important role the sports writers play. He never adhered to the concept most well-known athletes follow—if they just spell your name correctly, the newspapers are doing you a great favor you couldn't pay for. A printed slap was something which had to be answered immediately, whether the writer was in Tokyo or in the same car with him. Lawton Carver, former sports editor of the International News Service, used Hogan's by-line over an article without getting Ben's permission. Three days later, Lawton couldn't even recall what this grave misdemeanor was that infuriated Ben so. It just wasn't that important to him. But he was quickly to learn that it was *very* important to Ben! As soon as the column reached Hogan in Fort Worth, the little man was on the long-distance phone, ripping mad.

"I didn't even know what he wanted," Lawton said. "I picked up the phone and Hogan was on the other end. 'This makes me mad as the devil,' Ben said, and I had no idea what he was talking about. We talked for a while, more or less at cross-purposes, and then hung up without reaching any conclusion." Today Carver can't recall what it was that made Hogan so angry. But you can be sure that Ben remembers that long-distance call word for word, even though the incident took place eight years ago. When he wanted a column to appear under his name, he'd write it himself!

On many occasions, Ben has stepped into some hot feuds over the use of his by-line. Newspapers and wire services, as well as some magazines, frequently interview an athlete, write the story in words closely resembling his own, and then get an okay to use the man's by-line. This is helpful both to a golfer and the paper or syndicate. Ben usually doesn't go in for this kind of "ghost writing." In the early days, some of the newspaper boys just wouldn't take no for an answer. This irritated Ben and he raised the roof. Newspapers, magazines, syndicates, wire services, and others heard from him—or his lawyer—when they ran his by-line. The newspaper boys would tell me about it, and some of them would be hopping mad and ready to give Hogan the going-over of his life, in print. But such minor storms always blew themselves out, to everyone's advantage.

Bob Brumby, now a good friend, was another who once felt Ben's wrath. In 1942, before Brumby had met Hogan, he was working in New York for the newspaper *PM*, where he'd heard a lot about Hogan's manhandling the press. The stories rankled Brumby so much that he wrote a column in which he said that "Baseball has a press fighter in Ted Williams and now golf, of all sports, has an uncooperative star in Ben Hogan."

A month or two later Bob met Hogan for the first time at the Winged Foot Country Club in Mamaroneck. Ben stood his ground and gave the writer an icy stare. "No kidding," Brumby told me, "he looked as if he were about to reach for his six-shooter." The writer went more than halfway and offered Hogan equal space in his paper to write nasty things about him in return. The offer was rejected. "No, forget about it," Hogan answered, and the incident was closed. Since then, Brumby has become Hogan's good friend.

After many of us had talked to Ben about his habit of skipping out on the awards committee and leaving reporters empty-handed for stories, he forced himself to stop running. But even then he couldn't keep out of trouble. Out in Denver a couple of years ago, he finished up the last round of a tournament early. On this occasion, it appeared that five or six others, who were still playing, would certainly post better totals than his. Lew Worsham, Freddy Haas, and two or three others, including myself, were still on the course and were far ahead. So Ben went back to the hotel and packed. But in one of those strange reversals which crop up in every sport, all of us blew up along the back nine and Hogan's seven-stroke deficit suddenly became a one-stroke victory. He was leaving the hotel for Salt Lake and the next tournament when the call came through that he had won. It was too late to return to the course, so Ben just kept going. When he saw the stories from Denver the next day, he would have started shooting if he'd had a gun. He began putting in phone calls all over the place.

Ben used to remind me of a mole, the common garden variety that digs deep into the ground whenever approached by man or animal. Even on the street or in a hotel lobby, he didn't seem to have two words to spare for either friend or stranger. He was all business twenty-four hours a day— his mind constantly at work on the next shot, the next hole, the next tournament.

But this running stopped with the accident. For a while they thought he wouldn't live, then that he'd never walk again, finally that he'd never play another round of golf. It was a different Hogan who left the hospital that day at El Paso. He was glad simply to be alive. The changes in a man that a brush with death can bring about are pretty hard for most of us to understand. Suddenly he found that all this running was simply leaving him out of breath. He'd get back to the top of the golf heap, all right, but without running. He began to take time out for the little things. . . . Three years later, after he won the British Open, a press conference was held for him in New York which was attended by a couple of hundred news and television reporters. The room in which the interview was held was a sweating, stifling hot box. But Ben sat there, amiably, and went out of his way to answer any and all questions. As the tiring hour-long interview broke up, I heard a reporter remark, "He's certainly a changed little guy. Why, I remember how mad he got back in 1946. . . ."

Ben changed when he found out that life was pretty wonderful if you could just live it without pain and fear. It altered his whole attitude toward people. He found out that people truly cared about him. The flood of letters and telegrams he received while in the hospital gave Ben, for the first time, an inkling that people aren't so difficult to meet and get close to after all. I recall one line in the movie of his life, "Follow the Sun," which showed so clearly his old attitude. In this scene Ben and Valerie were talking about the new house they had just purchased and Val went into a little description of the house and the neighbors. "Neighbors? . . . Oh, you mean people," he said, glumly.

Today Ben has a legion of friends, people he goes out of his way to see and a step or two farther to help. This situation is just a natural development of his personality. Hogan always liked people. He enjoyed listening to the chatter of a golf mob, but there was always something which held him back and wouldn't allow him to step out and grab a man by the hand and say hello. He had an inferiority complex about people. He always felt that he was foisting himself on them, that the only reason they would talk to him was because of his success as a professional golfer. That's the sort of deep-seated complex much too difficult for me to explain. Perhaps you have to go back to the hard life in Dublin, or his first day as a caddy, to come up with the answer.

But he's over that now. It's standard procedure for Ben

to sit around after a tournament and chew the fat with the boys. And he's made a lot of friends doing it, too. What would appear, at first glance, to be a strange combination —Ben and Toots Shor—is one of the closest friendships in sports. Toots is a corpulent, gregarious gent whose New York restaurant is synonymous with sports and sportsmen. His first love is people and having a good time, and his loud voice during a sports argument can be heard down at the Battery although his eatery is on 51st Street. Hogan, in the old days, would have shied away from the place completely —too many people, too much talk, too many hands to shake, too many people who wanted to slap your back. Yet the first thing Ben does when he hits New York is to pick up the phone and call Toots, then hustle over to eat and talk with the sports world. Toots proudly displays a pair of cuff links with a St. Christopher medal engraved on the face of each link —a gift from Hogan.

"He's the most thoughtful guy around," Shor says.

Perhaps it was at Shor's that the change in Ben's attitude toward people became permanent and final. Toots threw a big party for Hogan in 1953 the day he arrived back from winning at Carnoustie. As he entered the restaurant, Ben, for the first time in my memory, seemed on the verge of tears. The people at the bar turned and clapped and then upstairs just about every important figure in sports arose and gave him an ovation as he entered. He had a lot of trouble making the words come out that day and his eyes glistened with tears. After it was over, I spotted him walking slowly through the crowd, making sure he said hello to every familiar face and some that weren't so familiar. Ben had learned, once and for all, that he had a lot of people on his side. It meant a great deal to him and he said as much in his little talk. He continually showed his gratitude throughout the huge welcome he received in New York. He seemed embarrassed that people should make such a fuss over him, but he acted the perfect example of a gracious champion. Why, he loosened up to such an extent that he cracked a joke now and then. He even borrowed a gag of mine in advising Shor about his golf game. "As Jimmy says, you're just a victim of circumference." People laughed. Hogan smiled. Things had changed.

Ben has become a generous fellow. Now I don't claim that he, or any other golfer for that matter, is the world's greatest philanthropist. Most of us had to do without for enough years so that we will never entirely forget the value of a dollar. But Ben has a fine streak of generosity in his nature which showed up clearly after the U.S. Open in 1953. I heard this story at second hand—Ben would never tell me—but I believe it to be true. After winning the Open, Hogan learned that his caddy, a boy named Stanley, was toting golf bags to raise money for his own college education. Ben promptly doubled his already considerable tip.

Each year Ben plays in a number of matches for worthwhile charities, donating his time and services free of charge. One such match at the Merion Country Club outside of Philadelphia I shall never forget. It was in July of 1951, and Bob Hope and I flew down to Merion in a small private plane to join Ben. The 1 P.M. starting hour rolled around, the crowd swelled to a mob, Hogan paced up and down on the first tee, but Hope and Demaret were nowhere to be seen. We were rocking about 10,000 feet above the Pennsylvania landscape in a severe storm. Meanwhile, to pacify the impatient crowd, Ben gave the spectators a free lesson, hitting ball after ball off the tee and explaining his shots.

An hour later, Hope and Demaret made a sensational entrance—in a cornfield next to the course! We had persuaded the reluctant pilot to land his small one-motor Cub on a Merion fairway, but at the last moment he picked an adjacent cornfield and down we came like the original reaping machine, scattering corn in all directions. As we hopped out of the plane and headed for the course, each of us grabbed an ear of corn. On the first tee, where we found Ben grumbling and looking disgustedly at his watch, we bowed low and presented him with two ears of corn. We were still somewhat shaky and green around the gills, but Katharine Cornell herself couldn't have staged a flashier entrance. Ben was so surprised he forgot to bawl us out for being late.

One element in Ben's life has never changed, in good times or bad, before or after the accident. That is Valerie, his wife. When you talk about Ben Hogan, you are talking about Valerie Hogan too. She is as much a living part of Ben as a wife can be. They met at the ripe old age of twelve, and have been inseparable ever since. Valerie is everything Ben Hogan needed to help him to the top—sweet and understanding when things weren't going well, strong and reliable when Ben needed moral support so desperately. After winning the Open in 1953, Ben made a little speech at the presentation ceremony and in the middle of it called for Valerie, who was, as usual, just mixing with the crowd in the background. "This is my trainer and partner," Ben said. "When I leave the golf course I put myself in her hands. She's the reason I won today. I have no other worry except my golf game. Valerie takes care of everything else. Thanks, Valerie."

With that, Valerie Hogan did a strange thing for her, and walked to her husband's side. She doesn't like the idea of stepping into the center of things. She has stubbornly remained in the background, out of the limelight. "I feel that Ben is the one who should get any laurels," she says. "I don't deserve anything and don't want anything." Even when her husband was being honored by the whole city of New York, Valerie managed to look like the least important person in the crowd. She has the real gift of humility.

Valerie Hogan is the kind of mild and retiring woman who makes it tough on anybody trying to capture her personality on paper. She is a quiet and thoughtful person, the type who leaves the impression that there is plenty going on—but all inside. She is a far cry from the wives of many celebrities— the loudmouthed and gushing sort whose main occupations are muscling in on the limelight and spending their husbands' money. Today, with Ben among the top sports heroes of our time, Valerie hasn't changed a bit from the shy, attractive girl I first met years ago.

She is an average-sized woman with brown hair and large brown eyes that do as much talking as her mouth. Her whole life is wrapped up in one thing—being with her husband. Yet her interest in Ben's career hasn't helped her own golf game one bit. By her own admission an impossible duffer,

111

Valerie tried golf for a time but gave it up before it drove her insane. "One golfer is plenty in the family and besides, I just can't play," she admits.

Valerie's marriage to Ben is one of the happiest and most secure I know. They seem to live only for each other. Partly because Ben and Valerie have no children, wherever Ben goes, his wife can follow; there are no separations, no matter where Ben has a playing date. Yet despite the enormous amount of traveling she does, no one gets more car-sick than Valerie. Perhaps it's a mental hazard, but she just can't ride in a car and feel well. "I keep swallowing those drugstore remedies all the time we travel," she says with a smile, "without much success."

At a tournament, you can usually find Valerie near the scoreboard in front of the clubhouse. She never follows her husband around the course in a match but would rather just sit and wait for him. But no one doubts that she plays an important part, even when he is a mile or so away sinking a 20-foot putt.

Photographs of Valerie are few and far between simply because she remains in the background so constantly. The only time I can recall her being in the middle of things was at the hospital in Waco. There, on a twenty-four-hour basis, she sat by her husband's bed, for once in the center of the stage, as the whole sporting world waited for news of Ben's death or recovery.

Valerie recalls her first meeting with Ben clearly. "I remember saying to myself, 'Oh, he looks so small.' But he grew up a little." As for those silly questions reporters ask about what is the finest thing about her husband (what do they expect her to answer—"His putter"?), Val answers in a simple statement which sums the whole thing up. "I love him, you know."

Ben's perfection on a golf course is apparent in many aspects of his personal life. He likes everything "just so." When in a restaurant, I call him the Ziegfeld of the menus. If a waiter brings a steak that isn't done exactly the way Ben specified, he takes the offending piece of meat back with specific orders for the chef: try again. Just as he charts a golf course, this little man goes over a menu. He's strictly a meat and potato eater, but more than one hotel has had him in the kitchen giving the chef some definite orders on how to fix his meal. "He's never done it here because we know what he wants and there are no mistakes," Shor told me. I remember an eating incident with Ben in Indianapolis years ago. Ben wanted a steak medium rare and an order of home-fried potatoes. The waiter, quick and efficient, brought back french fries and a crisp black well-done piece of beef. Then he disappeared, as only waiters are able to do, before Ben could object. He figured Ben would give up and eat. Instead, Hogan sat patiently for a few minutes waiting for him to return. Then he quietly picked up his plate and walked into the kitchen. He returned ten minutes later, with a medium-rare steak and some home-fried potatoes. He had apparently stood at the chef's elbow.

That dogged perfectionist attitude can be seen even in the way he dresses. His clothes are quiet and expensive. On every occasion he's as neat as a pin. Even his cigarette holder these days is a handsome item of alligator skin. In his attitude toward other sports, there is that same quality. I've seen him sit and writhe at a ball park when a major-leaguer swung and missed a pitch. Ben has a theory about hitting baseballs; he'd like nothing better than to get a batter and work on him to prove it. "They jiggle the bat too much," he says. His favorite ballplayer, appropriately enough, is that calm and poised professional, Stan Musial.

Although he has no baseball protégé, Ben is developing a young golfer, Gardner Dickinson, to follow in his footsteps. Oddly enough, this Dickinson, a lad in his early twenties, not only swings a golf club like Ben but even looks like him. I hear that Hogan has Dickinson out on the practice tee three or four hours a day down at the Tamarisk Club in Palm Springs, and Ben himself told me that "the kid likes to practice, Jimmy." I guess Ben wants somebody labeled "Hogan's kid" winning the U.S. Open in five years, and who can blame him? There's no finer way for a man to perpetuate his name than by passing along his talents to another.

It is in a business deal that you see the shrewd side of Ben Hogan. Companies seeking endorsements from Ben realize that they must pay the most because they're after the best. He only endorses products he knows to be the finest. His search for perfectionism in Hollywood, when Twentieth Century–Fox was making the "Follow the Sun" movie, almost caused Director Sydney Lanfield to jump from a bridge. In the first place, Ben refused to sign a contract until the movie was finished. He just didn't want his life misinterpreted and he personally was going to make sure it wasn't. He stayed right there in Hollywood, most of the time on the set, bothering the life out of everybody. "That doesn't look

114

like me at all," he'd say; "I'd never do a thing like that!" Glenn Ford, who played Hogan's part, really had his work cut out for him. When the movie people got exasperated, Ben would tell them, simply, "I don't need this. I can go home to Texas and forget all about it. I have no contract."

He drove everybody nearly mad. Halfway through the affair, they set out one of those camp chairs with "technical adviser" written across the back and sat Ben on it. That was right up his alley. From then on, the movie was practically Ben's property. All he needed was a beret and sun glasses. He completely ran the show. I know because I "acted" in the movie. My frank opinion, after sitting through a viewing of the finished product, was that he should have left the job of directing to the Hollywood professionals.

But you had to respect his attitude. This was the story of his life and Ben wanted it to be accurate. Despite his run-ins with the director, he made such a hit with Lanfield that the latter flew to Carnoustie to see the final rounds of the British Open. There is something about the plain guts and stubborn honesty of the man that wins the admiration of even those he is opposing.

Another thing has become apparent since his accident. Ben has a deep respect for the one Being who is a lot bigger than all of us combined. "I couldn't have done a thing—I wouldn't even be alive—except for the help of God," he said. Ben is following religion closely these days. Not in any stuffy manner, but in the coherent, deep faith of a person who knows what the Lord did for him.

CHAPTER 6

LIFE ON THE TOURNAMENT TRAIL

(*The Road to Psychiatry*)

I've been around golf courses all my life. They are the Demaret answer to the world's problems. When I get out on that green carpet called a fairway and manage to poke the ball right down the middle, my surroundings look like a touch of heaven on earth. Every blade of grass is a friend, and that good clean air seems to peel years from my age and pounds from my waistline. The rest of the world, with its noise and problems, is far away.

But put me on that same green and beautiful course during a $10,000 professional golf tournament and the whole situation is different. The trees seem to have grown arms that reach out to knock down a good wood shot. That innocent-looking trap to the right turns into a yawning, bottomless ditch. That bunker on the fifth breathes fire. The eighteenth green bucks and pitches like a ship in a storm. When I'm playing in a tournament, every inch of the golf course becomes my worst enemy.

There isn't a modern-day professional golfer—Ben Hogan

included—who can play in a big-money tournament with casual ease. The tournament trail is one of the cruelest of all sports grinds. In the old days, a professional golf tournament was little more than a friendly outdoor convention, and the fellow who could walk seventy-two holes in a straight line won it more often than not. Today's tournament trail—"the tour," with such flashy events as the Los Angeles and Kansas City Opens and Chicago's Tam O'Shanter—is one of the main events in the world of sports. In many ways it is an alluring setup which attracts more and more young swingers into golf for a "living."

Whenever those tanned, well-dressed pros appear on the course to chase a cash prize from $2,000 to $20,000 around seventy-two holes, a lot of people in the audience look wistfully at the spectacle and say to themselves, "Boy, what a life! That's for me. Why, take Demaret, for instance. Looks as if he hasn't worked a day in his life. He's living high." And when Ben Hogan or Cary Middlecoff or Lloyd Mangrum finishes up the last green a winner and walks up to the microphone and television cameras to accept a four-figure check, it must convince the fans once and for all that the life of a golf pro on the big-time circuit beats the custodian's job at Fort Knox. Well, sometimes I have to agree with this rosy picture, especially when I've just planted my feet solidly in the winner's circle. But there are many other days when I think a nice safe and sane job in a Houston department store would be a lot more attractive, and certainly more restful!

Something like this attitude prevails among all golf professionals, I think. Anyone who has packed up his clubs week after week, hopping from town to town and golf course to golf course, can tell you of the thrills and heartaches of golf tournaments. But, like Demaret, they remember the thrills more clearly. The tournament trail is a gaudy road lined with the best times a man can have—if he's on top. But if he's just one of the crowd, putting in the pick-and-shovel work on this uncertain road to success, it is far and away the toughest haul in sports. The winning tournament players are the ones whom people associate with the golf tour; it is the experience of the few steady winners that might suggest that the tour is nothing but a soft and fragrant bed of roses. But that is only the brighter half of the story. The other half is what often makes the tournament trail the road to psychiatry.

Approximately 150 professional golfers start out each January on the major tournament tour at Los Angeles. From there, they move along to just about every sun-bathed glamour spot in the country, with approximately 37 tournaments slated for the normal year. Along with the sun, these 150 professionals are following $750,000 in prize money, an amount large enough to hypnotize not only the experienced money-winning favorite, but also the empty-walleted youth with only a set of secondhand clubs and a strong pair of arms to recommend him. A man could do a number of things with even 10 per cent of that enormous figure. But it is deceiving. Of those 150 touring pros, only 10, on a yearly average, come away showing a decent profit after playing literally hundreds of rounds of tension-filled golf. The travel, the living in hotels, the insecurity, and the constant pressure on the course can make an old man out of a young player in a big hurry. When Bobby Jones quit golf at the age of twenty-eight, he told people that he was an old man. He meant it.

Yet, despite the obvious drawbacks, the tournament trail is one of those strange ways of life which gets in your blood. I call myself a semitour man right now. I play in only a few selected tournaments each year, as does Ben Hogan. But I could never really get away from them completely. Every once in a while, I'll note a rich stake and an exciting tournament coming up and, like the old fire horse, I begin to limber up on the tee, play a few practice rounds, and make mental notes about how long a trip it is to Miami or Long Beach or Chicago. I have pretty sound economic reasons for keeping my hand in this way. The tournament trail has been more than kind to Jimmy Demaret. Take 1947. I came away with $27,936 that year in prize money alone. And the two years which bracket '47 weren't exactly lean ones, either. In 1946 I won $19,406 and in '48 I earned $23,699.

In my case, the tournament circuit was the shortest road to financial success open to me, although those early years, as I've indicated, were somewhat barren of both dollars and applause. But because I was able to eke out victories in such events as the Masters and the Miami Open and finish in the money in 27 tournaments during 1947, I was lucky enough to become what you might classify as a "big name" in golf. The same goes for Ben Hogan, only more so. The little man has had some terrific years on tour. In 1953 he made enough money out of golf to start his own currency. But the fact remains that for every Demaret and Hogan there are a hundred pros who wind up borrowing money to make it back home after the tour. But the chances are good that they'll be back next year, trying for that jackpot. It's hard to get the tour out of your blood.

This tournament trail, along with everything else in golf, has been a steadily growing proposition. The tour today stretches across the country from California to Florida and even to Havana. While we still consider the "Winter Tour" as its true name, it has mushroomed into a fifty-two-week-a-year proposition. Its beginning is at the Los Angeles Open, held at the Riviera Country Club in the first week of January—always an auspicious start for the winners, for prize money is $20,000. The winner receives something in the neighborhood of $4,000 and the next five finishers all pull down four-figure checks. Then the tour packs up and heads to other California courses: to Monterey Peninsula for the Bing Crosby Pro-Amateur and its $10,000 lure, and to Long Beach and the $10,000 Lakewood Park Open. From California, the pros go to Arizona and Texas for the Phoenix, Tucson, San Antonio, and Houston Opens, all $10,000 or better events, and then on to Florida and the rash of Sunshine State tournaments. From there, we work up to Augusta and the Masters in April and then on to the National Open in June.

But that doesn't end the season. You won't see a pro packing his clubs away as long as there is a $25,000 first prize waiting for the winner of the "World's Championship" which they run at Chicago's Tam O'Shanter in August. And while he's up in that neck of the woods, the pro will have a go (as Bobby Locke would say) at the Canadian Open and then the Western Open. Thus, in the course of a year, the touring pros travel the length and breadth of the entire country—Texas, California, Oklahoma, Kansas, Ohio. Whereever they go, crowds line the fairways to watch them play. Money and fame await the man with two or three days of hot golf in his system. Each one of the 150 pros thinks the same thing each year, each tournament. "This time it could be me."

Over the years, the tournament trail has had a lot of fine builders and promoters. Golf has been lucky in this respect. It has attracted smart people who have built professional tournaments into what they are today. Three men especially, in my opinion, have done professional golf tremendous service in their time. They are Bob Harlow, the late Hal Sharkey, and Fred Corcoran. Veteran golfman Bob Harlow is now the editor and publisher of *Golf World* magazine at Pinehurst, North Carolina. Back in the twenties, Bob managed the colorful Walter Hagen and saw to it that the wonderful Haig was on deck for almost every major tournament. Just his appearance was enough to insure the tournament's success and give a lot of other people ideas about sponsoring new and bigger competitions.

But the father of the modern tournament trail for professional golfers was Hal Sharkey, a Newark, New Jersey, newspaperman. Before Sharkey devoted his attention to the game, tournaments were few, far between, and poorly organized. There was really no such thing as the tour, no major league for golfers. Sharkey had a heart ailment, which later claimed his life, and in 1928 he decided to heed his doctor's advice and leave Newark for warmer climes. At the time he was writing up golf news for the *Newark Evening News*. But aside from his typewriting talents, he had a pretty sound notion of how to promote a product.

Sharkey left Newark with the idea of promoting golf firmly planted in his mind. Fortified with weekly retainers from *The New York Times* and the *New York Herald* to cover all golf news in Florida and California, he packed up and journeyed west to develop that potential gold mine he saw in his favorite sport. He proposed to the somewhat surprised Professional Golfers' Association that wherever he could arrange new tournaments for the pros to play in, he was to receive 10 per cent of the total purse money. Of course he had to raise the purse money, too.

At the time, that 10 per cent appeared to be one-tenth of nothing, and the P.G.A. went for the idea with tongue in cheek. It took Sharkey about two years of steady traveling and talking to chamber of commerce heads, to city public relations directors, and to merchants' associations before the results became apparent. But after Sharkey had laid the groundwork, the pros had a total of $140,000 in tournament prizes to shoot at and the gold rush in golf was on. Sharkey had convinced many cities of the obvious advantages, from the economic viewpoint, of holding an annual golf tournament. The job he did still benefits us today. Quite a few of the prizes I've picked up over the years are a direct result of Hal's vision and hard work.

While Sharkey was making his points with the civic bigwigs, a young fellow from Boston who had packed more than one bag in his day as a caddy was working on the tournament circuit as everything from general errand boy to score poster. This was Fred Corcoran, who directs the tournaments today. Fred put his proper Boston accent to work for the good of golf, with clever emphasis on the publicity angle. To most newspapers the golf tour was a minor matter before Corcoran began to buttonhole such sports editors and writers as John Kieran and Joe Williams. He showed them that there was plenty of excitement in those local $5,000 tournaments and that the U.S. Open didn't constitute the entire game of golf. Fred became the man-around-Shor's, talking up the game, interesting people in it, keeping his eye peeled for a likely-looking sponsor. As far as the papers were concerned, he did everything but set the type for the day's links results.

"Sometimes I think we did too good a job," Fred says today. "A tournament used to be a simple thing. Get the course, a sponsor, and the players and then wait to see who wins. Today, it's a six-figure nightmare of parking prices, concessions, crowds, publicity, hotel reservations, and I don't know what all. And it never ends. We're here today and in St. Paul, Minnesota, tomorrow."

The present trend seems to be away from the event sponsored by the local chamber of commerce and toward big industry-backed tournaments. Beer and ale companies, for instance, are stepping into the picture as sponsors and as prospective sponsors. We now have a $20,000 Blue Ribbon Open put on by a Milwaukee brewery. Other individual businesses are finding out the public relations and promotional value of a big tournament is priceless.

Perhaps the most fabulous sponsor of them all is Waco F. Turner, the Oklahoma oil millionaire. They call him "Golf's Giveaway Man," and not without good reason. Waco runs the Ardmore Open at the Dornick Hills Country Club in Ardmore, Oklahoma, and for the past two years he's wrestled with a perplexing problem. He began the Ardmore Open in 1952 on the premise that he wanted to give *everyone* a prize. Turner is a former schoolteacher who struck oil in his neighborhood and picked up golf in 1917 when he was stationed at Fort Sam Houston, Texas, as a doughboy. He never gave up the game and even entered some tournaments in the 1930s. Today he is golfdom's answer to Santa Claus.

Ardmore is a small town, and until Turner approached the P.G.A. Tournament Committee in 1951, no city of its size had ever held a spot on the major tour. When Turner became president of the Dornick Hills Club, two prominent state amateurs, Charlie Coe and Bo Winninger, reminded him that the Sooner State didn't have a major golf tournament. Why didn't they try to set one up in Ardmore? The ordinary purse and guarantee for an event of this size is $15,000. Waco was able to raise the money in a matter of hours. Then he talked to the club's board of directors and the next day the bulldozers and construction men were on their way to Dornick. The entire course had to be remodeled and put into top shape for a major tournament. Greens were smoothed, traps increased, the fairways resodded and reshaped and a lake placed in the middle of one of them. The remodeling cost Dornick Hills $44,000, but there was more to come. Turner wanted a better-looking pro shop for the event. He had one built.

Dornick then hired a top-flight pro, E. J. (Dutch) Harrison, and scheduled the tournament for April, 1952. But Turner still wasn't content. He wanted to devise a new way of distributing prize money to more people. At the local minor-league baseball games, Turner had been in the habit of offering bonuses to players who delivered well—a free suit of clothes for a home run, a hundred-dollar bill for a shut-out, six gross of ping-pong balls for a double in the ninth inning. He saw no reason why the pro golfers in his Ardmore Open shouldn't have similar opportunities for augmenting their incomes.

Turner and his wife Opie worked out a list of prizes that offered a cash award for everything but missing. They put up $250 for a hole in one. On the last day of the tournament, they increased it to $500. A birdie was worth $5 and an eagle was good for $10 the first day, $25 the second, $100 the third, and $250 the fourth day. A hot round under the Turner plan would give a fellow enough money to pack up and go home to bed for a year. All through the tournament the Turners never stopped putting up lists of "suggestions" for winning more money. The low scorer each day won $100. If you cracked Ardmore's par of 70, you got $5 for every stroke under par. Then, to cap the excitement, the Turners told Dutch Harrison he'd receive $6,000, double the regular first-place money, if he won. Well, Harrison didn't win— Dave Douglas took that first Ardmore Open—but the Dornick Hills Club handed over $26,000 in cash to the pros for four days of golf. And they haven't changed their policy. In fact, they're still disturbed about the players who don't win. "Sometimes young golfers have to borrow money to get out of a town after a tournament," Turner complains. "I'd like to see to it that every man who steps onto the tee in the Ardmore Open goes away, four days later, with expenses and then some. And I don't care where they finish." That, gentlemen, is the sponsor of sponsors.

Of all the tournaments put on in this country, some richly endowed with tradition and others just richly endowed, I guess you'd have to call the "World's Championship" at the Tam O'Shanter Country Club in Chicago the Santa Anita Handicap of golf. There is a $25,000 first prize waiting on the eighteenth green for the winner. Just about every pro able to walk would enter this one even if it were played over the South Side garbage dump. (Every pro, that is, except Ben Hogan, who has been known to pass it up.) Tam is a fine course and a true test of golf. May, a prominent Chicago engineer and construction man, wanted the richest tournament in the world for his town and now he has it. The second-place finisher receives the small sum of $10,000 just so that he won't feel too badly about not winning.

In last year's Tam O'Shanter event, I came in a fair ninth and won $2,000. I finished early but came back to the last green where Harry Wismer was handling the radio and television announcing. Harry asked me to say a few words about the tournament and pretty soon, not being the bashful type, I was giving the folks a running commentary. It seemed certain then that the fellow standing alongside me, Chandler Harper, was about to win the first prize of $25,000. I was lavish in my congratulations. Harper is a fellow who has been dogged with a lot of tough luck on the circuit (or so he tells you) and he wanted to win this one in the worst way. Out on the eighteenth fairway was Lew Worsham of Oakmont, the last golfer who could possibly tie Harper. Lew was 125 yards off the green and had to get down in two to tie.

126

"I don't think he'll be able to do it," I told a few million listeners and televiewers. "He's just too far away."

Well, Worsham swung with that wedge of his and the shot came straight for the green. It was an impossible thing, I said to my radio audience. It just wasn't going to go in. It's a brilliant try, but just not quite enough. . . . The white pellet, as if guided by radar, landed on the green, skipped, hopped, and disappeared into the cup for an impossible 125-yard wedge shot and victory for Worsham. In my astonishment, I said something unprintable into the microphone. Harper, suddenly the runner-up, stuttered, sputtered, and nearly fell over. "There it goes—I lose again," he wailed. "I can't get a break. This time I'm giving up the game for sure. Look at that! Right in. Why does it always happen to me? There goes $15,000!"

The tournament circuit has its share of "characters," as you might imagine, but none more unique than a fellow we'll call Leo. This colorful gent—the son of a man prominent in early golf circles—is the intimate friend of millionaires, is well known by every golfer on the tour, is present at almost every big tournament, and has no visible means of support. His main interests in life are free food, free refreshments, and free lodging. On the tour he is known as The World's Best Sponger.

Leo's playing career is rumored to have consisted of one tournament, in which he defeated Byron Nelson when Nelson was at his peak. Although Leo rarely plays a complete round today, he is an absolute wizard on the putting green. One of his sources of income is enticing an unsuspecting golfer into a putting contest at high stakes and then cleaning him. His main source of income, however, is his unequaled ability to sponge—charmingly. He signs any one of a dozen names to his bills, names of millionaire sportsmen, oil tycoons, department-store owners. Even I have received bills from Havana, Bermuda, Puerto Rico—with my name written across the bottom in Leo's fine hand. And his tastes being strictly refined, those bills come from some of the finest hotels and restaurants in the country.

One of Leo's special friends is Frank Stranahan of the Toledo Stranahans, none of whom have ever been known to spend a day in the poorhouse. Two years ago, Leo was driving the Stranahan Cadillac from California to Miami and at some tournament along the way he promoted one of those special putting contests to raise a little money for himself. His adversary became so annoyed with Leo's boasting that he upped the stakes to $1,500. Leo readily admitted he didn't own such a sum but, pointing grandly at Stranahan's Cadillac in the parking lot, said, "I'll bet you my car." His opponent agreed and promptly outputted The World's Best Sponger all over the practice green—a feat rarely performed, I assure you. Without hesitating, Leo reached into his pocket, flipped the keys to Stranahan's Cadillac to the winner, and jauntily walked away. A few days later, the police and Stranahan's lawyers straightened the situation out.

When we tell people about Leo, we're always asked the same question—why do you let him get away with it? One answer is that Leo has charm; he's fun to have around. But more important, Leo has become a tradition, a landmark, a legacy in golf. He just sort of comes along with the game.

The players themselves can be classified roughly into two groups—the attractions and the entry fees. This might seem a harsh way to describe the difference between those 10 or so top golfers who come away from the tour showing a profit and the other 140 who go home with indigestion and empty pockets. But it is, sadly, the truth. Freddie Corcoran puts it this way: "Whoever signs up the top ten or twelve names in golf runs the sport. If you don't have these people—the attractions—at your tournament, there's no sense having one. And nine out of ten times that group will walk off with most of the prize money, anyway."

With so few actually making a living at it, the competition on the tour is fierce. Consider, for a moment, the little item called living expenses. These can set you back a cool $3,500 in an average year—and that's if you live close to the vest. It's true that Ben Hogan occupies a lush suite at a major tournament and it might appear to the outsider that he's living like a king. Well, he is. But that's Ben Hogan.

What about Ansel Snow, a young assistant of mine, who won only about $1,500 after two long years on the circuit? Those tours cost Ansel a lot more than he cares to think about—and he wasn't living in any fifty-five-dollar-a-day hotel suite either. "Snowball," as we call him, is thirty years old, a navy veteran, and a graduate of the University of North Carolina. No finer young fellow ever dug up turf— but he just doesn't seem to be able to win golf tournaments. He is unmarried, fortunately for his slim purse, and he picks up a little money teaching during the summer, but his life on the circuit is strictly a matter of squeezing dimes and pinching pennies. The traveling golf pros, like everyone else, must live according to their incomes. That doesn't mean there's a caste system among us. It's just that the individual bankrolls make a tight little caste of their own. They divide the winning players from the ones you rarely hear of.

But no matter who you are, life on the circuit is by no means easy. Constant travel, living out of a suitcase, playing four-night stands at a hundred different hotels—this could never be called a simple life. And even the winning players have to watch expenses carefully. Those fancy Florida events, for instance, are usually played at the height of the resort season. Those sky-high hotel and restaurant prices remind me of Louisville on Derby Day. Usually you can exchange a few shares of General Motors stock for a cup of coffee and a ham sandwich.

I could give lessons on how to be a winning golfer and still go broke on the circuit. I had a fair year on the tour in 1940. I won the Oakland Open, the San Francisco Match Play Tournament, the Western Open, the New Orleans Open, the St. Petersburg Open, and the Masters Tournament. That's a lot of tournaments to win first money in. But the catch is that the cities where I played were mighty interesting and entertaining places. In Los Angeles, never a dull place, I had myself as gay a time as a man can have anywhere. New Orleans has always been long on charm, and when that championship came my way down there it was only fitting that I should live up to my station in golf. Let's just say that I lived well, and leave it at that. The same goes for St. Petersburg. Demaret, the top tournament winner, ensconced himself in the bridal suite of the best hotel in town. I ate steaks that were 6 inches thick and took an occasional sip of Scotch that must have come out of the barrel when Robert E. Lee was a youngster. Well, the end of the whole affair came at Miami, where I did *not* win the Open. I found myself politely asking a certain friendly gentleman for a fresh bankroll with which to get the Demaret frame back to his house and wife in Texas.

Now, maybe this is a pretty out-of-the-ordinary example of free spending, but I assure you that it can be done quite easily. Eleven solid months of travel on the tour today can leave a man with a severe case of the financial shorts. The pros usually try to stay at one spot—a hotel where they can get reasonable rates. But even with these so-called "pro rates," only beachcombers can live cheaply in a place like Miami in the winter.

While on the subject of hotels and hotel bills, it might be pointed out that there are a frightening number of places in this country where you still have your pick of one hotel, take it or leave it. And if you take it, you're in real trouble. I call those places the "slim and none" hotels. That means you have two chances of getting a decent night's sleep and neither of them is too promising. There is one old place in Indiana—it's still standing, or rather leaning—which I'm sure can't be equaled anyplace in the world. I stayed in it *one night* during a tournament in 1949 and the minute I got up into my "room" I knew there was trouble. I don't want to say that there were bugs in the place, but along about one in the morning the walls began to get a little exercise. The whole room was crawling.

Then I had a second-story room in a Pennsylvania town once which was smack on the railroad tracks. Along about three in the morning an engine pulled onto the siding under my window and let out a cloud of good black, sooty steam. It came through the open window over my bed and left me looking like the third man from the end in a minstrel show.

The pros usually make the run from tournament to tournament by car, and the bachelors double and triple up. There are a large number of married boys in golf today, and over half bring their wives along. That makes for even heavier expenses, and a fellow with his wife in tow has to be a powerful big winner in order to live comfortably. As a rule, the whole golfing gang gets together only at the course. The younger swingers stay at private rooming houses or at motels and their food stoking is done at diners. The better-known veterans have friends in almost every golf town. People seem to want to meet us and certainly we want to meet them. Often they open their homes to us and usually have a local night club or two they want to show off. We make not only friends this way, but—to put it bluntly—valuable business contacts. A golfer's active career can't be as long as that of a business executive and we've got to look to the future. Golf is a grand old introducer.

This "attraction" business carries right down to the tournament's play. I remember too well those cold gray mornings I was forced to tee off at 6 A.M. just as the lesser-known players do today. The starting times are fixed so that a top gate attraction is scheduled to tee off at ten or eleven in the morning, when the cash customers will have arrived. The unknowns get their chance when nobody but the sparrows is watching. But once you tee off, no matter what your name or status, you face the same problems, physical and mental, as the two-one favorite. You have to get over the same sand traps, putt on the same greens, even fight the same nerves. For a younger player, this tournament grind is an invaluable experience. There is no better test of your golf than the seventy-two-hole pressure of a first-flight tournament.

In this regard, I always remember the case of Al Besselink, a fine young player who is now winning his share of tournament loot. Back in 1946, Al was a room-service waiter at the Vinoy Park Hotel in St. Petersburg. As a complete unknown, he entered the St. Pete Open, and on the opening day he got up with the early birds and shot in the sixties. Al figured that surely Christmas had come early that year. He had finally learned golf's secret. He went to Grantland Rice, who was staying at the hotel, and asked Rice to use a little influence in his behalf so that he could play with Byron Nelson the next day before a big crowd. Granny took care of the "pull," and Nelson's gallery took care of Al. They all but threw Besselink off the course when he folded completely and came home somewhere in the eighties. It was a tough lesson, but Al learned well, as his standing today indicates.

Most of the younger pros do not have the expense money to go on the tour and—as it happened in the cases of Jimmy Demaret and Ben Hogan—financial backing usually comes from somebody else at the start. Today, if a young assistant pro at a club shows promise and has the desire to make the tour, a few of the wealthier members get together and advance him the expense money to go out and try his luck. This is subsidizing the boy, I admit. But the best he usually gets from such an arrangement is meal and travel money. This is all most of the boys want, anyway, and I consider it a fine and honorable system. The young pro then plays as a representative of the course from which he comes.

The better-known pros earn a lot more in golf than just the tournament prize money. There are several other ways of making a living from the tournament trail—all depending to a great degree on the amount and quality of golf you play. The big three sporting-goods companies—MacGregor, Spalding, and Wilson—each pay a considerable amount of money yearly to various professionals for endorsements and other promotional stunts. Almost every set of clubs made, you'll notice, has the signature of a "name" pro written somewhere on the club head. The companies do this on the theory that the average Sunday golfer wants to give himself every advantage, and one such advantage is fine equipment. Perhaps, too, he even seeks to pattern his game after that of a certain pro. The golfer whose name is used will play with this model club on the tour. For this, he receives a royalty fee from the sales of the clubs. A few of the more industrious golfers even do their own club designing. Toney Penna, one of the game's best designers, developed the superior Penna wedge. My old clubmaking days in Texas left me with a fair knowledge of the business and once a year I spend some time in the MacGregor factory working with their production people on new ideas.

The golf-shoe business is another source of income. Many of the top pros are signed to contracts with shoe companies. We pose for ads, sign endorsements for a particular shoe model, and, believe it or not, even wear the shoes. The same goes for slacks, sweaters, and shirts. I have been connected

134

with companies in these lines for a number of years. Clothes (some might even say "loud" clothes) are a hobby with me, and today I serve on the Palm Beach Company's board of directors. A few years back I helped to design a special golf slack for golfers with middle-age spread. My enemies say that I modeled for it but that's just a nasty rumor. Not a word of truth in it.

In all the years I've been on the tour, no one ever broke in with greater impact than a country boy from Virginia, Mr. Samuel Jackson Snead. Ben Hogan, with his sheer artistry and near-perfection, has knocked the golf world cockeyed. But for that fine side-line humor that means so much to us on the tense tournament circuit, I've got to cast my vote for Slammin' Sam. Oakland, California, in 1937 was the scene of Snead's historic entrance into golf and I doubt if anybody involved has ever forgotten it. So many stories grew out of that first tournament of Sam's, which he won with a 270, that today the occasion reads like an expertly written movie script.

Sam came fresh from the Virginia hills where he was a crack athlete. He brought with him one of the finest natural swings golf ever has seen and he put it right to use in the Oakland Open's first round. Newspapermen and golfers alike were astounded when this newcomer ambled in with an amazing 67. They were even more amazed when they began to talk to Snead. At the clubhouse, after his historic round, Sam sat with a Coke in his hand while the news writers pumped him for information. Sam answered something like this:

"Well, lessee. Yup. Ah hit that tee shot right down the middle 'bout 250 yards, then Ah hit the second shot right smack at the pin, and then Ah had a short putt there and Ah dropped the little old ball right in. That's how Ah got that birdie on the sixth. Yup."

Fred Corcoran, who was watching over this little tableau with a paternal eye, went over to Snead afterward to educate him.

"Look," he told the Virginia free-spender, "the next time you have a round like that, if you ever have another, offer those writers a drink right away. They can give you a million dollars' worth of free publicity. They're not asking for handouts, but you make sure to offer them a drink."

The next day Sam shot his second wonderful round and once again, Coke bottle in hand, he was surrounded by unbelieving sports writers. He answered their questions as best he could, and after a few minutes Corcoran began tapping his foot impatiently and moving his elbow in the old "buy a drink" sign.

But Sam didn't get the sign. Later he told Corcoran, "Ah thought you meant when *you* weren't around!" Sam was born with a natural ability to keep his bar bills as low as his golf scores.

After Snead launched his colorful career with that Oakland victory, Corcoran showed him a copy of *The New York Times,* whose hallowed pages had dutifully recorded Snead's feat. The story read just fine to Sam, but it was the picture which bothered Our Hero. He gazed at it and then looked again.

"That's me all right, Fred," he said to Corcoran. "Sure

Ben and the author have been playing golf together for a long time. Here a younger Hogan and Demaret dunk straws in the same glass of milk at Augusta in 1940 (*Acme Photo*).

The same pair six years later, in the Miami Springs Country Club locker room, wear victory smiles after winning the International Four-Ball Tournament (*Acme Photo*).

A gaunt and weak Ben Hogan, after his terrible automobile accident in February of 1949, had to overcome many obstacles on the road back to golfing success. This is a photograph of Ben taken six weeks after the accident in the hospital at E. Paso, Texas (*Wide World Photos*).

Ben is helped aboard a train for Fort Worth after almost two months' hospitalization (*Wide World Photos*).

enough mah picture. But how'd they ever get it there? I never been in New York."

Such moments are fun to remember. Thirty years from now I'll still be sharing them with my fellow golfers, the newspaper boys, and the fans. They're an important part of what makes the tour a fascinating and wonderful way of life. The locker room after the final round of a tournament, despite the disappointment that must be there, seems to take on a New Year's Eve glow when the winner arrives. He receives congratulations from everyone, and then buys a drink or two for the boys he's just defeated. Suddenly the locker room is rocking with laughter. This honest comradeship between golfers, in many ways one peculiar to the sport, is one of the reasons why I love golf so much.

Seldom in other games do you find rival players helping each other as golfers do, sometimes even at their own expense. Before most any tournament, you can find some pro working with another, helping him to cure that fatal hook or that troublesome slice. You'll see a Cary Middlecoff standing out there on the practice green showing an Ed Oliver why he is missing so many putts. You'll see a Jimmy Demaret on the practice tee, listening to a George Fazio and trying to get more distance with his woods. And after the tournament, there's enough handshaking going around to supply three political conventions. The fellow who beat you out of $1,000 by one stroke is the best friend you have. And if you've been a steady loser and feel like calling it quits and heading for home, one look around the country-club locker room is reminder enough that you've got a lot of friends in the game who'd like to see you stick it out. Instead of quitting, you pack up those clubs and head for the next town. After all, it only takes one hot tournament and you're made. And that hot one could be coming up next week.

Golf is a great leveler. For a lad who never finished high school, I've met some fine people and visited some interesting places. Along the tournament trail, I have been privileged to play at some magnificent clubs and have been entertained at some fancy places. But when I finally quit competitive golf, it will be the friendships which I shall value most highly. At Detroit's Plum Hollow course, for instance, I have played a number of rounds with Henry Ford II and C. E. Sorenson, the father of the automobile assembly line. Both play the game as if their very life depended on it. Robert A. Firestone is another enthusiastic golfer I met out at Detroit. In 1946 we teamed up to win the LaGorce, Florida, Pro-Amateur and had a fine time doing it. On the golf course, Firestone has to hold up under a steady ribbing about the unique offer he once made to pay off a golf debt with a set of automobile tires.

One thing I always notice when playing with these industrial leaders is their inability ever to forget their business completely. Maybe that's what makes them such successes; their concentration on business amounts to complete preoccupation. As an example, take Robert W. Young, the railroad man. In the middle of a match he once asked me, rather absent-mindedly, whether I rode the Chesapeake and Ohio. The man must know that the C. & O. doesn't run any place near Houston.

Another business tycoon crazy about this game of golf is

138

Alvin Handmacher, a dress manufacturer and a special friend of mine. Alvin is a heavy-set fellow with a big heart and he's been bitten by the golf bug with a vengeance. He even puts golf into his advertising budget. The Weathervane Women's Cross-Country tournament, from which all receipts, amounting to some $200,000, go to charities, is sponsored by Handmacher's line of women's suits. He worries and fusses over this single golf tournament as much as he does over his entire dress and department-store business.

One of the more interesting men I've played with once set England on its ear when he decided the girl he loved meant more to him than being king. The Duke of Windsor—David—is a good 90 golfer and has the rare faculty of accepting his scores for what they are. He knows 90 is about the best he can do and he doesn't make himself unhappy trying to break it.

Golf opens other doors in the sports world. Every time I hit a major-league baseball city, I seek out friends like Dan Topping, who owns the New York Yankees, or Ted Williams of the Boston Red Sox or Cleveland's fine pitcher, Bob Lemon. One of my closest friends in baseball is Gus Mancuso, and if they've developed a better catcher since he retired I want to see him.

Another group I've always felt close to are the newspaper boys. I don't think a single member of the fourth estate will object to my singling out Grantland Rice as the sports writer who has done the most for golf. In fact, you might even say that Granny is the sports writer who has done the most for sports. Granny just doesn't grow old. He's been a sports writer and columnist for over fifty years. When he graduated from Vanderbilt almost half a century ago, he went to work persuading skeptical newspaper editors that football, tennis, and golf were sports worth covering and that prize fighting wasn't the *only* athletic activity deserving of sports-page space. Every American golfer—from Willie Anderson to Ben Hogan—owes Grantland Rice and his fellow sports writers a locker room full of gratitude. In the final analysis, it was the newspaper boys who made America aware of golf.

California is a state that has always been especially fond of golf. Particularly in Hollywood, golfers seem to find many friends. Two of my own favorites out there—who, incidentally, are acquainted with each other—are comedian Bing Crosby and singer Bob Hope. (Or is it the other way around? I always forget which one thinks he's funny and which one thinks he can sing.) Bob and Bing are old friends of golf. They play in charity matches, entertain the professionals on the Coast tour, and give generously of their time and energies to golf. In 1948, for example, the Western Golf Association sponsored an instructional film on caddying which was also to draw the nation's attention to certain college scholarships available to bag-toters. Bob and Bing jumped at the chance to donate their million-dollar services to this cause, free of charge. They not only appeared in the film but supervised its production.

Bing's private tournament for charity, held annually on the Monterey Peninsula, is one of the high spots of every tour. The tournament, paid for from start to finish by der generous Bingle, is, for me at least, one part golf and two parts party. In 1985 I'll attend Bing's shindig leaning on a cane, sitting in a wheelchair, or flat on a stretcher. But I'll be there, Bing.

These golf-course friendships the country over have paved the way, on several occasions, to business investments outside of my golf world—some sound, some disastrous. I doubt very much if many of my successful colleagues have been able to refrain from dropping a few dollars down an oil well someplace. Besselink, Lawson Little, Cary Middlecoff, and Lloyd Mangrum cashed in on one of those beautiful gushers last year. I have, on more than one occasion, hopefully invested a bit in a project which was drilling through good Texas earth for some of that better Lone Star oil. However, all we've struck thus far has been talcum powder. I won't bore you with stories of my other solider investments. Anyway, I reserve the softest spot in my heart for that dry oil well.

Although I usually don't drag my wife along to the tournaments, about seventy-five of our touring pros do make the circuit with their wives, and that's a life by itself. The lot of a golf wife on the circuit is a lot different from that of one of those week-end "golf widows" so many people speak of. A professional golfer's wife sits around and waits, too—but since hubby is out on the course for a living, not for fun, she can't exactly charge him with neglect. While a tournament is going on, the women usually camp in the clubhouse, developing their knitting and gossiping styles. Without housekeeping or cooking chores, the biggest job a wife has on the circuit is keeping her husband's spirits up after a bad day on the course. That isn't an easy job. A lot of golfers carry the day's outcome right to bed with them at night and even one quiet word from the Missus can produce a "you tend to the knitting, I'll do the putting" blast from the old man.

The wives rarely follow their husbands around the course. My wife Idella gets too upset when she comes out to see me play a crucial round. She stays at the club or at the hotel writing letters and keeping those buttons tight on my shirts. Valerie Hogan stays away from the course, too. "Ben wouldn't notice me, anyway," she says. At least twelve of every twenty-four hours, of course, the wives must put up with golf talk. Since my whole life has been devoted to the game, it's natural that with almost every visitor we have at home I begin to talk golf. If Red is trying to concentrate on who murdered what in "Dragnet," she'll finally yell in exasperation, "Golf room next door!" We'll take the hint.

The circuit is a pretty hard life for a girl to embark on, and it takes a lot of plain courage to stick it out. Endless travel from spot to spot and then the waiting and more waiting while the man in the family is out trying to make a living with his brassie is about as far removed from a normal married life as anything I can think of. But nothing can be more difficult than a couple making the circuit with a baby.

When our daughter arrived on the scene, Red retired from the circuit and stayed down in Houston with her mother. But there are several couples who pack bag, baggage, and baby into a car—although they really need a truck—to travel the tournament trail. Dick Mayer, a promising young pro from Greenwich, Connecticut, and his wife Doris, did it last year with their five-weeks-old son, Dick, Jr., in a station wagon. But even a first place in the Eastern Open at Baltimore didn't

142

keep matters from reaching a complicated stage for the Mayers. By the time they reached the Ardmore Open in Texas, packing and unpacking the station wagon had become infinitely more difficult than winning a mere golf tournament.

On the last day at Ardmore, Doris was to pack and leave the motel, pick up Dick at the course in late afternoon, and take off for the next stop. Doris stayed up most of the night, carefully diagraming how she was going to fit all the paraphernalia into the station wagon. After testing her paper theory several times the next morning, she dutifully stuffed into the sagging station wagon her own and her husband's clothes, one portable icebox for the baby's bottles, one portable stove to heat them, one crib, several hundred diapers, a bassinet and collapsible carriage, and finally a load of baby-formula food and bottles. Quite pleased with herself, Doris got behind the wheel and drove out to the Dornick Hills course. Dick was just leaving the clubhouse when she pulled up in the station wagon. There could be little doubt that she had done a fine packing job. Only one item had been overlooked—a spot for her husband to sit down. Dick took one look at this moving van and headed toward the mob to bum a lift to the next stop.

Ben and Valerie at a major tournament keep to themselves most of the time. Rarely is he around with the rest of the boys. This does not mean that Ben has trouble getting along with people. It's just that Hogan, during a tournament, doesn't want to think about anything except golf. Ben doesn't play in all the tournaments today and hasn't since his near-fatal accident in 1949. He's no youngster any more, and despite his strong build he feels the complete tour would weaken him.

Some people have seen fit to comment critically on this fact. These snipers claim that Hogan picks his tournament spots carefully and that if he made the complete tour as the others do, perhaps he wouldn't be the unbeatable player he is in these special events. Day in and day out, the rugged circuit would take its toll on Ben—just as it does on every fine golfer. Over the tournament year, even the best have periods when a Sunday duffer could spot them shots and win.

Well, my answer to this criticism is simply that if the man is picking his spots, he's certainly picking the tough ones. A fellow who competes for the Masters and the U.S. Open, the P.G.A. and the British Open isn't laying off the pace and looking for soft touches. What Ben avoids are the wide-open Texas and other grapefruit courses where the sun has scorched the fairways and roughs to the point where the whole layout has become one big driving range. After you play under such conditions, it's difficult to get accustomed to the narrow fairways and tricky layouts of the Merion or Oakmont courses where Hogan competes.

While I'm gassing about the tournament circuit, I'd like to make a blunt and unsolicited comment or two of a general nature. Professional golf should get smarter in the way it handles tournaments. In the old days, tournaments used to be played on the nation's finest courses, but now, with the exception of such as the Masters and the Open and Bing Crosby's private event, they are played in the main on public links. The pros have been losing their invitations to play on the private links and it's not difficult to put a finger on the reason why. We are losing our good will.

Before every tournament starts, it is normal procedure to

hold a pro-amateur round or two so that club members can have the opportunity of playing a round with an experienced golfer. This is an important feature of public relations; after all, these gentlemen are paying for the tournament in many cases. All too often, I've caught pros glaring angrily at their amateur partners in utter disgust after these gents miss an 8-inch putt or blow up on the last hole. It is a stupid and disgraceful reaction on the part of the pro and I have little doubt that such incidents are the reason for so many private clubs recently turning down tournaments. Who wants to be insulted?

In two other ways, the attitude of the pros is damaging the game. During the pretournament practice rounds, I've seen experienced golfers, who should know and respect what a job it is to keep a golf course in shape, go out there and break every rule in the book, using regular greens for putting practice and generally working over the course as if it were to be demolished the next day. Then, when the tournament itself starts, play is conducted at a snail's pace. Some golfers today remind me of kids walking to school and praying they'll be late. Sometimes it takes players from four to five hours to finish a round. Such an unbelievably slow performance is a sure-fire way to make the gallery, who pay an admission price of about $3.60 for their slow walk, give up and go home. Golfers used to check the grass on the greens; today they study the roots under each blade. Gene Sarazen, when he made his annual appearance at the Masters recently, couldn't believe the slow pace at which the tournament was conducted and made no bones about his critical attitude. As an example of how slow play can demolish a gallery, Dick Chapman and

Frank Stranahan, two of our best amateurs, played a thirty-six-hole match in England recently and started out with 4,000 spectators. By the time the two boys finished up, the sun was going down and the gallery had dwindled to nothing.

The treatment of caddies is the last item on my complaint list. A caddy's job is difficult enough without having to wait all day for a player to finish. And when the evening shadows fall over the eighteenth green, he still gets the same fee as a kid who finished hours earlier. Tournament planners should see to it that there are rules to cover extra time put in by caddies. Too often we pros forget our own caddy days. One golfer who remembers is Lawson Little, who set up a college scholarship for his caddy the day after he won the Open in 1940. One method for measuring the importance of caddies is in terms of a golfer's tournament trail budget. Byron Nelson once estimated that his caddy fees totaled $5,000 in a single year and he wasn't exaggerating. If they are that important an item, they should be treated as such. A caddy today receives $10 for the day and usually a percentage of the prize if his player wins. That's the way it should be. But after one tournament recently, I regretfully remember the winner handing his boy exactly $12 out of a purse of $2,000.

Caddies produce a lot of the best humor in golf. I always remember a boy called Skeets, who caddied for Bob Hope for years. At the Rose Bowl a couple of years ago, I looked around and saw Skeets sitting one row back right on the 50-yard line. I complimented him on getting the best seat in the house and asked how he came across the ducat.

"Hope gave it to me," he answered.

"I guess he treats you pretty well," I commented.

"He darn well better," Skeets answered. "I've been caddying for him for ten years and he's never had a bad lie yet."

Wiffy Cox, an affable pro, had a wonderful caddy one year at Pinehurst, a bag-toter named "Snowball." Wiffy was a fellow who spent a dollar as if it were going out of style and when he came home first in the Pinehurst tournament, he turned around and put $150 into Snowball's hand. "Thanks, Snowball, I certainly needed that win," he told the boy. The next year, Cox returned and asked for the same caddy again. It was a whole day before Snowball appeared and even then the caddy seemed in a hurry to leave.

"I'm sorry, I can't caddy for you no more," he told Cox. "You done ruined my life. I got to leave now."

"Ruined your life? All I did was give you one hundred and fifty dollars, and that never hurt anybody," Cox replied.

"Oh yes it did." Snowball shook his head sadly. "It ruined me. I got married with dat money, and my wife she made me take a job."

A lot of people have asked me whether it's better to be a regular home pro at a golf club or to run yourself ragged on the circuit. It's a hard question to answer. Although the tournament professional usually plays as a representative of a course, he rarely sees his home base. The home pro, on the other hand, is that reliable fellow at your golf course who, day in and day out, takes care of your golf needs, helps improve your game, sells you equipment, and sees to it that there is plenty of golf activity going on at your club. The fellow in the pro shop or on the teaching tee is the backbone of the game today. His life may be less flashy than that of his touring brothers who make the headlines, but his occupation is an important and profitable one. Today, a home pro holds down a fifty-two-week-a-year job. In the old days, he often worked at two clubs, one for six months in the South and another for a similar period in the North. But now an active club serves golfers throughout the year and the pro has to stay close to home.

Al Ciuci of the Fresh Meadow Country Club on Long Island is a fine example of a successful home pro. Al made the tournament circuit a long time back, but he wants no part of it today. He started his present career on a public course in Yonkers, where he helped teach a fellow by the name of Gene Sarazen, and moved from club to club until he gained his present post. At Fresh Meadow, Al is a golfer, a teacher, a golf committee chairman, and a businessman. He gives lessons to members at a rate of $4 per half hour. He also sees to it that there are caddies and locker-room boys to take care of the members' equipment. As chief pro, he usually has two assistants who do most of the teaching. Often one of these assistants will take leave to try his hand at tournaments. The home pro's personality is a big factor, too. A touring pro can be a gruff and worrisome fellow and nobody is going to mind too much, as long as he irritates only himself. But when you're running a home course, you've got to be affable and easy to know. Nobody wants to play golf for leisure with a snarler or a complainer. Many of the former big-name tournament players eventually move into home pro jobs such as Ciuci's. Billy Burke, Claude Harmon, and Henry Picard are names which come to mind immediately.

It is a decision each golfer must make for himself. A home

pro leads a more sedate life, but he lives a longer one. I've been connected with clubs as a steady home pro for the past five years and leave them only to play in a few tournaments. I consider that a happy medium.

But either way, it's still golf. And it sure beats working for a living.

CHAPTER 7

WINNING EIGHTEEN UP . . . THAT'S FUN

The Ben Hogan you see on a golf course seems to be a stone-faced robot—something like an I.B.M. "Thinking Machine" calculating its way down the fairways with golf clubs. In a golf match, whether it be the British Open or a casual round with Jimmy Demaret, Ben is a gent who has divorced himself from the rest of the world. The only thing he cares about is making the next shot. Whether he's two strokes behind or twenty ahead, the shot coming up is the only thing that matters. When you compete against Ben, you are crossing clubs with a lot of golfer. I know that from experience. Playing hundreds of rounds with him, I've found out just how good the man is—and what makes him so good.

There is much more to Hogan's game than the shots he makes. Those 67s and 68s he always seems to be able to produce in the crucial round of a tournament are the result of a lot of things getting together in Hogan at the same time and busting loose out on the course.

Ben's hot rounds come from five different sources besides

just his superior ability with golf clubs; these are not clear-cut separate assets but in combination they are all but impossible to beat. In the order of their importance they are: (1) His intense determination to win. (2) A temperamental make-up which just doesn't have a letting-up point—the match is never over for Ben. (3) His complete concentration. (4) His quiet confidence in his ability to shellack you nine and eight. (5) More practice than any other golfer has ever taken. Add these intangibles all together and they spell out probably the finest competitive golfer ever to step onto a tee.

Hogan's refusal to let up, no matter what the score, was never better demonstrated than the time he and I won the Inverness Four-Ball Tournament in 1941. It was held in June on the Toledo course and we won the $2,000 first prize with a plus eleven. In one of the several team-against-team matches which make up this kind of tournament, Ben and I were doing very well against two fine golfers, Lawson Little and Lloyd Mangrum. We had a five-hole lead going into the back nine and the way things were going I just knew we couldn't lose. Ben was having one of those fine Hogan days—which means that his game excelled in *every* department—and Demaret wasn't slouching either.

I was feeling pretty happy along about the eleventh hole and I began to loosen up, singing a song or two, passing a few cracks around, chattering with my caddy. You know, sort of reminding everybody that it was actually fun to be out on a golf course. (And it's *great* fun when you see a $2,000 check coming your way.) But such fiddle-faddle in a match wasn't for Ben.

"Come on now, settle down," he instructed me. "We can

win this match if we keep going. You can have all the fun you want later."

"Aw, Ben, we're way out front," I objected. "We can't lose."

But the man would have none of that. "We're five up now," he snapped, "but what's wrong with winning by eight or ten?"

He's always like that. No matter how far ahead, he is grimly determined to get still farther ahead. The man likes nothing better than to have you nine down on the eighth green, then line up a nice 20-foot putt that will plop neatly into the cup and send you scurrying downtown to the hock shop with your clubs. His idea of a perfect day on the course is one in which he wins eighteen holes on every round—with all birdies and eagles.

Hogan practices more than a stage-struck tap dancer. When there's a tournament on, he is playing twenty-four hours a day. He doesn't leave his game at the country club but takes it home to bed with him. I remember the time we were playing in the Miami Open back in 1946. Byron Nelson and Ben were staying together in a room adjoining mine at the Venetian Hotel. There was a door between the two rooms which we left half open—for the first night, anyway. That particular evening I went out to give the town the Demaret once-over and came back to the hotel about 3 A.M. to settle down in bed with the morning papers. I was just starting to give them my usual close study, beginning with the sports pages and working my way back to the comics, when I heard this noise coming from the next room. A steady tap . . . tap . . . tap. Like somebody beating on the rim of a drum.

Ben is golf's hardest worker and takes the game very seriously. In typical surroundings, he hits a few dozen practice shots before the Los Angeles Open in 1950 (*Wide World Photos*).

Ben glares at the photographer who took this picture during the same tournament. Note the "No cameras please" sign. Ben has always been disturbed by cameras, and at one point during this tournament he threatened to stop playing if the photographers continued to take his picture (*Wide World Photos*).

Ben's 1953 victory in the British Open at Carnoustie Scotland, touched the hear and captured the imagination of the American public. He is pictured holding the British Open Trophy (*United Press Photo*).

Ben is welcomed back to New York by applauding crowds and a ticker-tape parade up lower Broadway, July 21, 1953 (*Wide World Photos*).

I wondered who thought he was Gene Krupa at that hour, so I ambled next door to investigate. I found Hogan standing in the middle of the floor clutching his putter, and Nelson next to him, giving instructions. Ben was stroking ball after ball across the rug and against the wall. Nelson told me he had been at it since dinnertime!

That performance wasn't unusual for Ben. In 1953's United States Open I was walking through the hotel after dinner when I met Ben en route to his room to "go to bed." You guessed it—he was carrying his putter.

You won't find other golfers doing things like that, because they don't have the tremendous will to win that motivates Hogan. We're all serious about the game, make no mistake about that, but Ben has the kind of determination that makes the rest of us look like carefree schoolboys. It's one of the big reasons why he is the greatest golfer ever to hit a ball.

I've always claimed that the intangible part of the game that goes on inside of Ben is more important than the part that is outside and clearly visible. There are golfers around today who have a better visible game than Ben. For instance, Hogan can't hit a ball the distance that a Sam Snead or a Roberto Di Vicenzo can knock off the tee. And I don't think he can match Nelson's accuracy as a driver. But on that "inside game" of his—the unbelievable will to win, the quiet determination, the intense concentration—Hogan tops them all.

His determination steam-rollers over every obstacle—and one of the biggest obstacles is nerves. Controlling your nerves is the key to tournament golf, and Hogan is the lifetime owner of that key. On the course every move he makes seems mechanical. He walks quickly from shot to shot, puffing on the inevitable cigarette. He takes a long time lining up his shots and longer than anyone I know selecting his clubs. He may make a little sign to the caddy when he picks out the club—you know, one of those "Do you think this is the right club?" gestures. But he makes his own decision. Then he hands the caddy his cigarette and steps up to the ball. He wastes little time once he has things lined up; he hits the ball quickly. Out of this calm, poised performance comes, more often than not, something the rest of us pros don't like to think about—one of those dead-to-the-pin Hogan shots. Then the gallery applauds, Ben hands his club to the caddy and takes his cigarette in return, and heads for the next shot.

There's a lot more to this than meets even the imaginative eye. Ben has that "inside game" of his working overtime as he walks along. He is holding his nerves in complete check, turning on his determination and concentration. And he consistently refuses to go to pieces at crucial times, like so many of us do.

To grasp the importance of this emotional control, you must understand just what nerves mean in golf. The game is wrapped up in your ability to control yourself. The ball sits there on the grass, calmly waiting for you to hit it—or maybe I should say challenging you to hit it. This can be the most nerve-wracking thing in the world, this silent challenge from an inanimate object. You have too much time to think. To keep your hands from shaking and your stomach from getting butterflies in the middle of, say, a Masters, is the toughest job in sports.

It is nerve-wracking partly because of the stillness of it.

The experience of Joe Louis, who loves to get out on a golf course, is a good example of what can happen to an otherwise icy-nerved man when he opposes that silent little ball. Old Joe will tell you that he seldom was worried by a fight—and his record bears him out. Once he and his adversary traded the first punches, Joe didn't have time to be nervous. He was moving, the other fellow was moving, and there wasn't much time for worrying or thinking. If Joe had ever stopped too long to ponder about his next maneuver in the ring, he would have come to with the referee keeping time over his head. But when the Brown Bomber gets on a golf course—even in a dollar-a-hole match, and Joe has been known to bet higher—he literally shakes his way through eighteen holes, "choking up" on the greens as he goes. An opponent such as Buddy Baer, who weighed in the neighborhood of 240 pounds, never bothered him much. A 1½-ounce golf ball ties him in knots.

Ellsworth Vines provides another good comparison between the strain in golf and the tension in a faster-moving sport like tennis. Vines was a great tennis player a few years back and later he excelled on the golf course. But in golf he found things a lot different, so far as that "inside game" was concerned. "In tennis you seldom have a chance, once things get going, to get shaky," he says. "You're too busy running around like a race horse. But in golf—hell, it makes me nervous even to talk about it. That little white ball just sits there. A man can beat himself before he ever swings at it."

At Carnoustie, while shaking their heads at the amazing game Hogan displayed, the Scots dubbed him the "Wee Icemon," meaning he had iced H_2O circulating in his veins instead of blood. Let's explode that myth right here. Hogan has as fine a set of screaming nerves as anyone in the game. The difference is that he refuses to let them take over. Ben runs his nerves as smoothly as he runs a putt right into the cup. When superior golfers blow crucial holes and rounds, it's not because their shots leave them. It's because their nerves move in. But not Ben.

Ben's own words on the subject are these: "From years of discipline, I learned to control myself in a tight spot. But I can play best when I'm a little excited. I can't play my best round when I'm not keyed up." That is what I call Ben's "inside balance," the perfect even keel for an athlete. You're no good in sports unless you have that little bit of excitement running through you when an event starts. But you're worth even less if you can't control it and put it to good use. All Hogan's tenseness goes into determination—and then the determination beats down his nerves.

But he must wage a constant battle. In the 1950 National Open, played on the tough Merion Country Club course at Haverford, Pennsylvania, Ben started out on the fourteenth tee with what appeared to be another title in his hands. The best score turned in was a 287 and all Ben needed was to play the last five holes in par and he'd have a 285 and a neat two-stroke triumph. The gallery knew it, and 12,000 people surrounded him as he started on those last five holes. With everything up to Ben—and his nerves—he made his par on the fourteenth. But on the fifteenth, he lost the battle, putting nervously for a bogey. He fought back with a par on the next hole, but then completely fell apart on the seventeenth. Ben's iron shot was wide of the green and his shot from a bunker was poor. His putt was a weak little thing which stopped dead a couple of feet short of the hole. It was another bogey on a par-three hole, and it came at the worst possible moment.

If there was ever an obvious spot for Hogan to blow a tournament, it was there on that eighteenth. He'd just posted a bogey five and his lead had evaporated entirely. But this is the kind of spot in which Ben's iron discipline asserts itself. He wasn't kicking himself for the last two holes; he wasn't muttering in anger. He walked up to the tee for the last hole of the tournament in perfect control. He slammed a long drive and then a whistling iron shot to a good spot on the green. He knocked in his second putt, a tough one to make, for a par four and a tie. The next day he clicked off pars as if he were a machine, winning the playoff from George Fazio and Lloyd Mangrum.

Most golfers lose their composure when they come up with a bogey in a tight spot and more often than not they begin working on a whole string of bad holes. I have that habit myself. Everything will go smoothly until I hit that terrible hole, then—poof—my composure disappears entirely and the scorekeeper has to send for an adding machine to keep tabs on me.

At the El Rio Country Club at Tucson, Arizona, they have posted on the par-five eighteenth hole a memorial to my ability to blow up high, wide, and handsome. There is a wooden sign on the tee. On it is a simple "Jimmy Demaret took a fourteen on this hole." There is a stroke and distance penalty for hitting out of bounds. One day in 1947, I came onto the tee needing only a par for a 67. The first five balls

I teed off soared a mile out of bounds, all in the same direction. My accuracy was amazing. You could have covered them with a hat. As I bent down to tee up my sixth ball, Lew Worsham, with whom I was playing, leaned over with a reminder. "For your information," he said, "you are shooting eleven." To make matters worse, I got a birdie four with the ball I finally was able to play. On that terrible fourteen, I have no idea to this day what I did wrong. I was keeping my head down, I was concentrating, I wanted to win. After the first ball cleared the fence, maybe I began to press. Certainly I was pressing after drive No. 2 headed off in the same direction. By the time the fifth ball left the tee, and the course, I was seriously considering giving up the game. My only consolation was that I preserved my reputation for doing everything in a big way. When I blow, man, I really blow!

Faced with such disaster, the average golfer begins to talk about a run of bad luck. It isn't bad luck, brother, it's your nerves forcing you to press. Pressing belongs in a tailor's shop. When you start to press on a golf course, you might as well pick up for the afternoon. Even Hogan isn't Superman. Like the rest of us, he has lost championships because of three-putt greens. He blew the Masters to Herman Keiser when he three-putted the last green in 1946 and he lost the Open to Lloyd Mangrum the same way that year. He lost a chance for a playoff in the 1946 Open at Cleveland's Canterbury when he three-putted the last green and finished with a 285 for a fourth-place tie. As Ben walked onto that eighteenth green, he needed two normal putts to give him a

284 and a deadlock with Lloyd Mangrum, Vic Ghezzi, and Byron Nelson. Ben blew his chance when he missed his short second putt, a shot most amateurs could make on a good day. In the Masters in 1952, he started off the last round in a tie with Sam Snead for the lead. Each had 214, but Ben went all to pieces and took a 79 on his last round and slipped to seventh place. Snead's 72, for a total of 286, won the event. I'm not pointing out these debacles to tear Hogan down. I'm just showing that it can happen to him, too. It just doesn't happen very often, that's all.

On the green, Ben not only fights his nerves inwardly, but locks the gates against tension with what I call his "choke-proof" putting stance, a technique described in detail in a later chapter. He's an inanimate object—not a man—when he putts. For my money, he is golfdom's greatest putter from 8 feet or under. Mangrum and the South African Bobby Locke may be better on the longer ones, but from 8 feet to the cup it's hard to beat Ben and that locked stance of his.

Hogan approaches a golf tournament the way Jack Dempsey used to go into a fight. He says to himself, "This is going to be a tough one, but I'm going to win it. I'm going to make *sure* I win it."

Then he picks up his clubs and heads for the course, where he'll practice like no one else I've ever known. He loves to just stand there and hit golf balls. No man ever lived who has hit as many golf balls as Hogan. He won't think of going out for a round, even a meaningless one with friends, unless he's hit some practice shots. And practice for Hogan may mean hitting as many as a thousand balls in five or six hours. I consider myself as strong as the next fellow, but I'm fagged out after two hours of practice shots. Ben just stays out there and hits and hits long after I've trailed off to the showers.

In the first round of the Rochester Open in 1941, Hogan burned up the course, shooting a record 64. He had ten birdies in that score, but the poor guy took a six on the par-four seventeenth. I had a 69, which I thought good enough, and I sat around with the fellows in the clubhouse until it was almost nighttime, gabbing and having a drink or two.

When I went out to the car to drive home, I noticed a late evening eager beaver all alone on the practice tee hitting wood shots. I didn't have to be told it was Hogan. I walked over to him.

"What are you trying to do, man?" I asked. "You had ten birdies today. Why, the officials are still inside talking about it. They're thinking of putting a limit on you."

Ben gave me that dead-serious look of his. "You know, Jimmy, if a man can shoot ten birdies, there's no reason why he can't shoot eighteen. Why can't you birdie every hole on the course?" And then his face took on a look of real anguish and he wailed, "And how about that terrible seventeenth?"

After he won the Open at Oakmont in 1953, Ben told the crowd at the award ceremony that "adequate preparation and knowledge of the course are essential. I have to learn the course thoroughly." By that, Ben means he wants

160

to know the place so well that he could give a biologist a thorough life history of the four rabbits who hole up off the fourteenth fairway.

It's this knowledge of the course he is playing that enables Hogan to pull stunts like the one on the eighteenth hole in the 1953 Open. His solid drive soared 250 yards straight down the middle. Then Ben brought a groan from the gallery when his midiron shot went into the rough on the right of the green. The spectators should have known better. Ben doesn't shoot into the rough as obviously as that without some special reason.

"I knew the grass over there wasn't so high," he explained later. "So I went for it deliberately. You see, if I'd played the fairway, the bunker guarding the green might have trapped me. So I knew the rough was better—this time, anyway."

That is what you call a thorough knowledge of the course, gentlemen. The next shot? Oh, that was just a little old 50-yard pitch right into the cup, a sort of stroke of death for "impossible" Oakmont and that year's Open.

Ben is particularly effective playing on the country's tough top-flight courses. Such a course, in my opinion, is one which is a true test of a golfer's ability but also is the beautiful product of a skillful architect. There are a number of courses which fit this description in America, places where every hole is both a challenge to the golfer and a delight to the sight-seer. You might wonder why I emphasize the scenic angle here. Well, as far as I am concerned, a golf course should be a thing of beauty. I can't rate a course as top-flight if it is composed of sand, gravel, and railroad tracks. It may be a challenge to pitch across railroad tracks or putt through a gravel pit, but who wants to try it?

Consider the Augusta course, for instance. Its fairways demand a skilled artist to do them justice. Yet they are narrow and treacherous when you attack them with a golf club. As for a single extremely difficult hole, there is none worse than the sixteenth at Cypress Point, California. This 240-yard par-three hole is a peninsula jutting into the Pacific Ocean. The green is framed by the white foam of the ocean breaking on the rocks. Out of bounds along the fairway demands that a man be a strong swimmer if he wants to retrieve his ball. The changing atmosphere along the shore is another factor to contend with here. I've used a four iron to reach the green in the morning and in the afternoon found myself short with a driver and nine iron. The wind kicks up at any moment and from any of a number of directions. In the 1952 Bing Crosby Pro-Amateur, the average score was five on this par-three hole. Lawson Little took a fourteen and Henry Ransom an eleven. Ben Hogan carded a seven on this notorious sixteenth. The wind and waves were good to me at Cypress Point in 1952 and I managed to win the tournament.

Just a mile and a half away from Cypress Point is another backbreaker, the last hole at Pebble Beach. This is where Harrison Johnson played his approach shot out of the ocean and put it in the cup to beat Doc Willing in the U.S. Amateur in September of 1929. As a blowup hole it rates with the best of them. The hole is 550 yards long and is a par five. The ocean is to the right of the green and there is a wicked dogleg to the left. Anybody taking a chance on shooting the ball over the trees and short-cutting that dogleg is running the risk of hitting into the ocean. Even the golfer who plays it safe and takes two full woods and an approach shot to go for the par has his hands full. One wrong move and his ball gets a salt-water bath.

Of course any hole can prove a crusher when the pressure is on. Sam Snead would have to rate the eighteenth hole at Spring Mill Country Club in Philadelphia as one of the worst. Sam needed a five to win and a six to tie in the 1939 Open and he proceeded to come blazing home with an eight. In my experience, that particular hole is not in the class with Cypress Point or Pebble Beach. But for Sam, who was dead set on winning that Open, a more treacherous hole never existed.

As a rule, Ben Hogan manages to save his most remarkable performances for the important tournaments. These are often played on the most difficult courses. As an example of the consistency with which he shoots under-par golf, over tricky layouts and under high pressure, let's compare his scores in the last four American Opens and the British Open with par for those five courses. (See the table on page 164.)

Practice is one thing most golfers dislike. It's mighty dull work. Byron Nelson, even when he was in the middle of that great string of victories in the late thirties and early

COURSE AND PAR			HOGAN					
		Par	Total par					
1948	Riviera *7020 yards*	71	284	67	72	68	69	...276
1950	Merion *6694 yards*	70	280	72	69	72	74.	.287
	Playoff	70	70				69	... 69
1951	Oakland Hills *6927 yards*	70	280	76	73	71	67	...287
1953	Oakmont *6916 yards*	72	288	67	72	73	71	...283
1953	Carnoustie *7200 yards*	72	288	73	71	70	68	...282
		Total par...*1490*				*Total strokes*...*1484*		

forties, never drove more than a dozen practice balls in one session. Sam Snead isn't the greatest man in the world for practice, and I frankly hate it.

But Ben just keeps on swinging from the practice tee. He has turned practice for a golf match into a long, gruelling and never-ending duty. In Portland, Oregon, in 1947, when he won that P.G.A. crown and broke nearly every scoring record in the official books, I don't think he ever laid his clubs down for more than an hour. On the last day, the field played thirty-six holes. Three down after the morning round of eighteen, Ben walked from the eighteenth green with Porky Oliver, his opponent. Old Pork Chops—we call him "Corned Beef" now since inflation has changed his eating habits—was intent on sinking his teeth into something solid and was heading for that clubhouse at a rapid gait. But Ben turned aside with a casual "I'll see you later," and headed for the practice tee and an entire hour of beating golf balls. In the afternoon, Ben went out in 30 to defeat Porky six and four and set the medal record at Portland with a 261.

At the next stop on that 1947 tour, Tacoma, Washington, they were still talking about Hogan's astonishing twenty-one strokes under par at Portland. But the first sight to greet the eyes of his fellow golfers at the Tacoma Country Club was Hogan on the practice tee taking a driving lesson from the veteran Ky Lafoon, the highly respected Oklahoma pro. Ben had hurried away from Portland so that he could profit from Lafoon's invaluable advice before the next event started. Apparently twenty-one under par wasn't good enough.

When he is practicing, you'd think Ben was knee-deep in a big-money tournament. Two years ago, the two of us played a casual eighteen-hole round over the Augusta National Course where we were to compete in the Masters Tournament later in the week. It was a nice April day and the course seemed like heaven to me. I especially appreciate the Augusta course, because they've planted a different type of flower in the rough on every hole and each one of them smells and looks prettier than the last. Incidentally, Augusta is the course Ike Eisenhower usually plays on. That's proof enough for me that he is a man with good taste.

Well, Ben and I were working our way along the eleventh hole when I hit a shot deep into the rough. When I walked in to find the ball I just stood there and took a deep whiff of the air and gazed at the flowers. It was good to be alive.

"Ben, don't you just love to get in the rough here?" I asked.

"I don't like to get into the rough *anywhere*," he snarled back. And I'm glad he stayed out of it, because he would have bitten the tops right off those flowers.

Ben carried his practice mania a little too far, for my tastes, when he was the nonplaying captain of the Ryder Cup team in 1949. The team is composed of the top U.S. professionals each year who play against the best the British have to offer. For me, a foreign trip is always a business and pleasure combination. I planned to play a little golf, relax, and see what makes Piccadilly Circus go around.

But when we got to Ganton, outside of London, where the match was to be held, the old Hogan practice bug had bitten. The man began to lay down practice rules the likes of which I had never heard in twenty years of golf. He scheduled exact practice times and special competitive practice rounds —all of them early in the morning—and even decided the number of hours we were supposed to sleep every night. You'd have thought we were in training for the Army.

The first day when I showed up for practice at about one in the afternoon, pretty early for me, I found Ben walking around the tee and sputtering. "Aren't you going to give this routine a try, or what?" he said to me right off. "You were supposed to play eighteen holes at ten o'clock. Come on now, Jimmy, let's get going."

"Aw, Ben," I told him. "I'm still operating on Texas time. It's only six o'clock in Houston right now and that's pretty early for me to be playing golf."

We kept up a running argument about practice and sleeping hours the whole time we were in England. I'd say the debate ended in a draw: I practiced twice as much as usual but

166

half as much as Ben wanted me to. In any event, our Ryder Cup team defeated the English professionals seven to five.

Ben's supreme concentration on the golf course sometimes causes unfortunate misunderstandings. People mistakenly think that he is snubbing them, when nothing could be further from the truth. After the U.S. Open in 1953, which he won by six strokes, Ben stopped into the bar at the Oakmont Country Club and had a victory drink. The whole golf mob, players, writers, and fans, were there, talking things over. When Ben saw the crowd, most of whom he knew, he seemed surprised. "Where's everybody been?" he asked, and began to shake hands and say hello to the boys.

Well, everybody he was saying hello to had been at Oakmont for four days, and a gent down at the end of the bar passed a remark about it. "I said hello to him the first day I got here," this fellow recalled. "If he'd pick up his head once in a while, he might see his friends."

It seemed like an appropriate remark at the time, but the man who made it doesn't know Ben Hogan. He doesn't ignore people. He just doesn't see them. Hogan simply divorces himself from the rest of the world when playing in a tournament. He is absolutely and completely detached from everything but that golf game of his. It's a common crack for golfers to say, "I played thirty-six with Ben today and the only thing he said to me the whole time was, 'You're away.'"

That is the Hogan method of playing golf. Since he's the man winning the tournaments, we can't criticize it. Everyone knows that a big item in golf is the art of keeping your head down when you hit the ball. Ben concentrates so much during a big tournament that he keeps his head down even at the dinner table. He doesn't see anybody and\ he doesn't want to see anybody. An old friend isn't going to do Hogan any good when he has a tough shot to make. But a long look at the green and another at his ball will.

One thing that used to spoil Ben's concentration was the *B-z-z-z-t!* of a movie camera. I remember standing on the ninth green of the Colonial Country Club course in Fort Worth in 1941 when a camera bug in the crowd pulled the trigger just as Hogan was leaning over a putt. Ben jumped up as if he'd been shot and then aimed a glance at that camera that probably cracked the lens. Later, when I asked him about it, he came up with a pretty solid reason for his violent reaction.

"Jimmy, those movie cameras always sound like rattlesnakes to me. When I was a kid, rattlesnakes used to scare me to death. I never completely got over it. When I hear that buzzing sound, I want to jump into the nearest tree."

A lot of times, inconsiderate and thoughtless people in the gallery will run up to Hogan and ask him, "How did you make that last shot?" when he's walking along the fairway. Ben will pass right by those people without even realizing that he has been asked a question. That isn't an insult. Rather it's the picture of a man working hard at his living. Hogan doesn't talk much at any time, but he's particularly silent during a match. He doesn't want somebody to tell him "Nice shot" four times a hole and he doesn't bother his playing partners with such amenities.

John Derr of the Columbia Broadcasting System was one of two American correspondents who went to Britain with

Ben to cover the British Open at Carnoustie in 1953. John became very friendly with The Hawk before the tournament, but he was lucky if he got ten words out of Ben during the whole affair.

"I just stationed myself in the middle of each fairway as Ben came down, making sure he could see me," Derr says. "Ben knew I was keeping careful track of how everybody else was doing in the tournament, and if he wanted to know, he'd walk over to me and I'd give him a run-down on the scores. Occasionally he'd come up and want to know how Locke or Stranahan or somebody was doing. But most of the time he'd just walk straight past me as if I wasn't there. I'm sure he didn't even see me."

CHAPTER 8

HOGAN'S GAME AS I SEE IT

There are two things in life which Ben Hogan especially dislikes. One is losing a golf match. The other is teaching golf. Even in the days when he had to give lessons or starve, Ben's heart was never in the business. However, the golfer eloquent enough to persuade Ben out on the course today for a little instruction would get the kind of expert advice which would go a long way toward cutting strokes off his game.

After a few hours with Ben, he would come away with a pretty good idea of how Hogan holds a club, how Hogan gets that special fade, how he charts a course and selects the proper club, and how he locks himself up for those deadly 8-foot-and-under putts. He'd also get a little touch of the Hogan "scoring-area" technique.

This chapter isn't intended to give the reader a thorough course in how to play golf in the Hogan manner. Instead I shall try to cover some of the basic features of Hogan's game and his special techniques for hitting certain shots. I have watched the man play hundreds of rounds of practice and tournament golf, too often against myself in hot competition. I have a thorough knowledge of just how he hits a golf ball and what constitutes his general approach to this game of golf.

THE GRIP

Every fine golfer, if he lasts for any length of time at the top, must have a sound grip. It is essential to have those hands of yours in the proper position every time you pick up a club. This can't be overstressed. Your two hands are the only part of the body that touch the golf stick. Each hand has a separate job to do, but they must work in perfect unison. No matter what the position on the club, the hands must be firm and free.

The grip Hogan uses today is a considerable improvement, you can be sure, over his technique in the early days, when he first swatted from the left side and then moved over and hit them cross-handed. Ben uses an overlapping grip, as I do myself. His left hand palms the club, with the club shaft's leather grip stretched across the palm a little above that tree-bark callus line of his. When Ben puts his hand around the club, the left thumb is on the center of the shaft. The pressure point for this hand is in the last three fingers. The right hand, which is the power hand at the moment that the club meets the ball, actually holds the club. The right hand's little finger is hooked to the big joint of the index finger on the left hand. When you fold the right hand over the club, you should have a little tunnel in the palm of the hand into which the left thumb should fit snugly. The pressure points for the right hand are at the forefinger and thumb, for myself, but Ben's grip puts the greatest amount of pressure *on the two middle fingers*.

If you hold the club correctly in the Hogan manner, an inverted V will be formed between the index finger and thumb of the right hand. This inverted V should point straight at your chin. The grip should always leave the hands relaxed, comfortable, but firm. Hogan's grip is as good a one as golf has ever seen, and with it he controls his shotmaking almost perfectly.

In the Hogan swing, there is a delayed hand action, which results in the power being turned on late, at the base of the swing. His right hand generates most of it. Instead of wasting a lot of power on the backswing, the little man applies it only when he's just about to hit that ball out of sight.

The grip described here is Hogan's normal grip. Naturally he has plenty of variations on it for special shots, such as a deliberate hook or a heavy slice to get around a tree or some other obstacle. Such shots are fine points which professionals have to spend a lot of time on. I would strongly advise the average golfer to learn to smack that ball straight and long with this normal grip. Then he should see the club pro if he feels ready for those advanced tricks.

I give this advice because, in my experience, a good golfer is not simply a natural—with the possible exception of Sam Snead, who was literally born to hit golf balls. Ability, strength, and mentality being equal, the fellow who studies his techniques and practices them steadily is the one who will improve. Over the years, even the top golfers change their way of doing things. In every department, from grip to swing, golfing techniques change and improve over the years. Ben Hogan has altered his entire style. Even in the middle 1940s, after he had reached the top, Ben modified his grip a bit.

HOGAN'S HITTING AREA

Next, Hogan would concentrate on your swing and here The Hawk would explain the real secret of exactly where the power comes from in his shots. One key to Hogan's swing is his ability to wait. He doesn't waste power on that backswing. Then, when the instant arrives for banging that ball, he has the *widest hitting area in golf*. When Hogan brings his club down for the ball, he brings it down in a wide arc. He drags the club along the ground in an arc so flat that it is almost a plane.

When he turns on the power, he is hitting through the ball. From this factor comes his distance. The average person's hitting area is a small arc at the base of the swing. The ball is approximately in the center of this arc, and his swing is aimed almost directly at the ball. This allows him only a small area both for hitting and for following through. Ben, on the other hand, gives himself plenty of hitting area. This, in turn, allows him to slam the club right through the ball. Instead of putting power into the swing the moment it begins, Hogan brings his swing down, flattens it out, and then turns on the power *at the last possible second*.

Hogan has some very definite ideas about "average" golfers which would undoubtedly affect this hypothetical lesson of yours. He once divided golfers who take lessons into three classes. They were (1) the player willing to work, take the proper instruction, and carry out the advice given him by the professional; (2) the player who is fairly good but won't do the necessary work to improve; and (3) the week-end trick player, who comes out to the practice tee to pick up a few fast tricks so that he can play at least passable golf on that particular Saturday afternoon. Ben once delivered a short, accurate, and none too charitable discourse on what he thought

A wide hitting area

about that third type. "He is not too interested and will always tell you that he plays only for the championship and exercise. His type is very prevalent, but I don't believe his apparent nonchalance toward his scores is honest. Anybody who plays is always concerned with his score, and the truth is this fellow just doesn't want to put in the effort to improve." Of his three classifications, Hogan stated honestly that he was entirely disinterested in the second two. "This hypothetical pupil," he concluded, "must be converted to that class that is willing to work to improve."

I tend to agree that *every* golfer, no matter how much he

denies his interest, really cares about his score. I've seen proof of this time and again at my Concord course. A fellow who shoots those telephone numbers out on the course will come back and say, "Oh, I don't care. Look at all the fresh air and exercise I got. So my score was a hundred and three. What's the difference?" Then, a day or two later, the same golfer will come into the pro shop all excited and jabbering away. "Jimmy, I shot a ninety-five today," he'll yell, as if I needed a hearing aid. "And I would have done better if I had any luck with my putter. Jimmy, tell me one thing—is my grip right?"

THIS BUSINESS OF FADING

In preceding chapters I've mentioned Hogan's left-to-right fade, which contributes a great deal to his on-the-fairway accuracy and keeps him out of so much trouble. From 1938 until 1942, Hogan hit the best ball I ever saw, as far as power and distance were concerned. But the little man was hitting with a slight hook, a right-to-left motion. His shots were low whistling drives, which, all too often, bounced into a bunker or a trap guarding the green. A hook has a habit of nose-diving into all sorts of trouble. Ben used to have as many as seven poor holes in a round—seven holes in which he found himself forced to shoot his way out of difficulty. To-day, using that soft fade, he comes up with only one or two a round.

Wild Bill Melhorn was the first of the faders, and after him Craig Wood and yours truly further developed his style. A steady golfer must get height on his shots, just as a basketball player must arch the ball into the basket. It stands to reason that a shot coming down from up high is going to bounce more gently and has a better chance of stopping dead roughly at the spot where you want it. But a low-trajectory, high-velocity drive may hit the ground and skip in any direction—too many times right into trouble. Ben often remarked about the way my shots dropped down on the green, instead

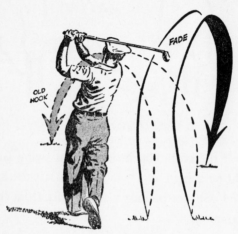

Hogan's fade

of bounding on and then off into traps or the rough. He was having trouble controlling his shots at that time, and a combination of Picard's advice and my example brought about Ben's decision to change that slamming style.

It must be made clear at the outset that this left-to-right shot is *not a slice*. It is just a slight fade. Hogan made some minor changes in his grip in order to develop it. He moved the back of his left hand *to a spot where it pointed at the line of flight* and placed his left thumb straight down the shaft instead of slightly to the side. With this change, the

176

inverted V's are pointing at the chin instead of over the right shoulder. His stance was opened a bit more and the left foot pulled back slightly from the line of flight of the ball. The fade is played off the right side and the club face

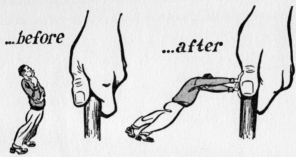

A slight change of grip

squared off at the ball. The product of a swing from this stance should be a high shot which fades left to right in a gentle arc and will not bounce a mile away from that spot at which you aimed.

THE SIMPLE SWING

A lesson with Hogan would include a lot on this fade, but he would make other comments on the manner of developing a smooth stroke. An important pointer would be to simplify your stroke. Today's tournament professionals have cut down the amount of motion and commotion in hitting a golf ball to a minimum. In the old days, even Bobby Jones and other equally fine golfers used a good deal of seemingly exaggerated movement when they swung. Their hips moved, their legs pivoted, their necks turned, and it seemed as if a dozen things were happening at once. Hogan, on the other hand, swings the club simply and directly. If you can get your club head, hands, and shoulders to move back at the same time and come forward simultaneously, then you have mastered a reasonable facsimile of the modern tournament swing. Forget about that movement of the derrière and about the rolling of the neck and the dozen other items people advise you to remember. When Hogan swings, he just moves those three items—club head, hands, and shoulders. The rest of the body takes care of itself. When he moves his arms and shoulders back, his hips will pivot without his having to tell them to. Some things just take care of themselves.

The simple swing

A word on this "keep the head down" business. It can be overdone. In fact, there is no doubt that it is just as bad to keep the head down too long as it is to raise it prematurely. The head will follow the movement of the shoulders in a good swing. It will rotate naturally as the swing begins and will follow the club right along to the ball. The head must be down at impact with the eyes fixed on the ball. But then don't strain to hold it there unnaturally. Just let those shoulders carry it right through. A head kept down too long restricts the follow-through and is a regular bank burglar when it comes to robbing power from the swing.

THE STANCE

Unless you've developed something mighty new and different, you hit a golf ball from a standing position. Thus the stance is an important item. The essential element here —again, it's simple—is to be properly balanced when you swing. It shouldn't take six chapters or a month with Ben to tell you that the only way you can judge your balance is through your own senses. When you place your feet in position for a shot—wider for a long shot, closer together for a shorter one—you can feel in a second if you are not balanced. Power comes from a firm, well-balanced golf stance. I never saw anybody yet who could hit a golf ball while jumping into the air or with one foot off terra firma.

If you watch Hogan, you'll see his right foot move a bit just before he hits the ball. That's an important element of his stance. When Ben lines up for a shot, he holds his body fairly rigid for a moment. While he shapes up to relieve this pressure, he makes a little movement—a slight shifting of his weight to the right instep for a moment. Then he digs in and swings his whole body into the ball with all the power at his command.

But any Hogan lesson would end with one thing we all follow today. Drive and strive for simplicity—and then play your own game.

That sackful of clubs your caddy is toting for you can be mighty kind to you, if you're using the right ones. Or it can cause you a lot of woe if you don't take the time to think a shot through and just grab any old club. Each one has a definite job to do on a certain area of a golf course. When you select the right club, you take the first vital step toward making a successful shot.

Watching Hogan pick his club amounts to watching one of the greatest club selectors in golf. He knows precisely what each stick in the bag will do for him. Although this is just another of the many things he does to perfection, he's always particularly impressed me in this department. He does everything that the average person should do and usually doesn't. He takes into consideration the wind, the distance, the obstacles, the condition of the course.

To begin with, here is a rough table that can be used as a general guide toward selecting the right club.

Club	Distance
Driver	From 240 to 275 and up
Brassie	From 220 to 265
3 Wood	From 200 to 250
4 Wood	From 200 to 225
1 Iron	From 180 to 215
2 Iron	From 175 to 205
3 Iron	From 165 to 200
4 Iron	From 155 to 190
5 Iron	From 145 to 180
6 Iron	From 135 to 170
7 Iron	From 125 to 160

Club	Distance
8 Iron	From 115 to 150
9 Iron	From 105 to 140
Wedge pitch	Edge of green to 105
Sand wedge	Edge of green to 40

This is, I repeat, just a rough guide. In many cases, you may find that a two iron just isn't enough club for you to hit for 190 yards. You may not command that kind of power. It's a simple matter then to go to your woods. Each player must choose his club according to the distance he gets when hitting naturally. When Hogan picks a club, he doesn't have to force himself to make distance with it. Nor does he baby himself on a shot in order to remedy overclubbing.

The weather and wind have a lot to do with the choice of a club. Other things, such as the texture of the grass and the amount of moisture both in the air and on the ground, count heavily. Take clover, for instance. If you see Hogan getting set for a shot from a clover patch, you'll note that he takes two clubs less than usual. That's because a ball skids or slides from a clover lie. The oily texture of the small leaves greases the club face when it contacts the ball, making it impossible to impart backspin. The ball will loop and float through the air with very little control. You might compare it to a spitball thrown by a baseball pitcher. It is because of such factors that we usually place club selection and course charting in the same category.

In selecting a club, it is often wise to seek the advice of your caddy—if you're sure he knows both the course and his golf. A lot of times, a bag-toter knows the course as well as the greenskeeper and has walked over it a thousand times.

A sound word of advice from the caddy here and there along the eighteen holes could spell the difference between a par and a birdie. But more important, the golfer must know his own game. He must not be ashamed if he needs a two iron to do the work of the four iron his partner uses. Golf is strictly a game of individual abilities. Even among the pros, a variety of clubs will be used on the same shot. A tremendous hitter like Sam Snead will use an iron while I'll still be on my woods. It doesn't matter what clubs get you on the green—as long as you get there in fewer strokes.

Consult your caddy

Ben has one technique in his club selecting which brands him a conservative. On an approach shot, he tries to make certain he is short of the green, rather than over it. At Carnoustie in Scotland, all the trouble lies behind the greens, as it does in 90 per cent of the courses here in America. Time after time during the British Open, Ben's caddy would finger a four iron but Ben would take the five instead and plant his shot a bit short but in a safe position. The caddy thought

Ben was wrong in playing it safe this way, and he wasn't the first one to have that idea. I remember a round with Ben at the Colonial Country Club in Fort Worth after which his caddy told the other boys in the yard that "I know more about this course than Hogan does."

During the round, from first to eighteenth hole, this bag-toter kept touting Ben on that one extra club. Each time Ben asked for the one under it. "You'll be dead to the pin with the four," the caddy said on one hole.

"I'll take the five," Ben answered, and planted his shot at the edge of the green.

"He would've been right up to the hole with the other club," the caddy muttered to me. "This guy is a champ and this is his home course, but he keeps using the wrong club!"

I just laughed. Ben Hogan knows only too well that trouble lies behind those greens. He'll take the club less and shoot for the front, and a sure two-putt green. Who's to say this conservative approach is the wrong one? Not me, certainly.

Course charting is automatic for the careful fellow who selects the proper club. When Hogan goes into the bag for a certain stick, it is a safe bet that he has looked over the area he is shooting for with a telescopic eye. He plans his shot carefully before swinging. A number of times he has been criticized for taking too much time with his shots. They call him the surveyor, and Ben resents it.

"That's a brutal word to tag on a golfer," he says. "When I look a course over, I'm trying to figure it out. I want to know what's going to happen when my shot hits the ground. I want to check the grass as well as the distance to the green or my particular objective. Now what's wrong with that?"

Absolutely nothing, is the answer, when a golfer is simply going about his business thoroughly and not just wasting time. It's one of the elements which makes a great golfer. Ben knows grass thoroughly—from that Bermuda green we have in Texas to the soggy turf of a seaside course. He knows what the ball will do on each type. He is the master attacker of even our toughest layouts, because of this ability to think out a course. If necessary, he'll pace off the distance from where his ball lies to the spot where he thinks it will come down. While he's doing that, he'll investigate the grass and every shrub, tree, bunker, and depression along the way. In the 1953 Open, he strolled 250 yards uphill on the seventeenth, to get an idea of what would happen when his ball hit the ground. Then he went back and laid his shot a club-length away from the green. If he's trying to whack that ball over trees to save ground on a dogleg hole or he feels that he can drive over a bunker, he always makes sure just what's behind these obstacles. He knows what's going to happen on the other end of the shot.

PUTTING

Course charting reaches its height of importance on the green. An illustration of the importance of reading greens occurred in the 1953 U.S. Open at Oakmont. The fellows were reviewing the bidding in the clubhouse after Ben won, and somebody ribbed him about an 18-inch putt he had missed on the seventh hole of his last round. Ben's answer came quickly and definitely. "It was the only time I got careless. I didn't read the green well enough. Serves me right."

When Ben gets on a green, he studies the contour, the grain of the grass. Ninety-five per cent of the time, the grain of the grass runs toward the setting sun. Naturally, you get more roll putting with the grain than against it. A green is a finely manicured piece of real estate and it reacts violently to rain or sun. Try putting a green when it still has a heavy morning dew on it, and you'll find it takes a strong stroke to propel the ball toward the hole. In the afternoon, however, if it has dried out, the same grain may be fast and tricky. As Claude Harmon always has maintained, reading a green is like reading the small type in a contract. If you don't read it with painstaking care, you are likely to be in trouble.

All greens have a break to them, either right or left. In other words, if you hit a ball straight across a perfectly flat green, somewhere along its path it will begin to swerve right or left, depending on the direction in which the bent grass urges it. Most greens are built on an uphill approach. Because of this fact, and because trouble lies beyond the green, Ben always tries to go a little light on his approach shot and place his ball on the front part (often called the "safe side") of the green. Frequently, a fellow with a strong shooting game will blast his shot to the back of the green and then must face the difficult task of chipping or putting downhill. The downhill putt is notoriously difficult to control. You will always find a careful golfer like Hogan shooting for the safe side.

There are a couple of standard tricks which can help you in reading a green. First of all, it is an advantage to figure out the direction in which the grain of the grass runs. About the best way I know, and the method Ben Hogan uses too, is to look for a shine on the grass when lining up the putt. If you see it, then you are putting with the grain and your ball will travel swiftly and quite a distance. If the shine is running from right to left, Ben would have you putt to the right a bit to offset the break to the left. The opposite would apply, of course, if the shine were running from left to right. A complex problem crops up occasionally when the green rolls in one direction and the grain goes in another. Ben would advise you to do as he does—give it some thought and then hit the ball straight, in hopes that the roll and grain will nullify each other and the ball will roll directly to the cup.

These are fine points which only your judgment on a particular green can solve. In a lesson with Hogan, you will pick up the rudiments of analyzing a green but you'll have to practice to learn how to apply them. Hogan has been doing it for years. All he has to do is stand on a green and the feel of the grass runs right up through his golf shoes to his mind. In my own case, I can walk across a green once and my feet will usually tell me how fast it is and roughly what its tilt amounts to. This is something you pick up only through experience.

Ben's putting stance is that locked-in "choke-proof" affair I mentioned earlier. He puts the index finger of his left hand over the little finger of the right in what can best be described as a reverse overlapping grip. (In the normal overlapping grip, the little finger of the right hand overlaps the index finger of the left.) All of Hogan's left hand is turned a full notch to the left. This tends to lock his hands, restricting any unnecessary movement. On this stroke, Ben keeps his head down all the way, barely moving it as his shot gets off. He keeps his eyes directly on the ball, and his concentration on the shot is nearly perfect. He doesn't move a muscle until he strokes the ball.

Head locked
to prevent
neck swivel
...

...head
braced
on chest.

The putting stance

The position of the feet must rely on individual choice. Balance, even in putting, is the thing to strive for. Normally, in what is called the square stance, the feet are spread evenly, with the ball in the middle. An open stance has the left foot slightly drawn back from the imaginary line of flight of the ball. A closed stance has the right foot drawn back. When Hogan putts, he uses the closed stance, with the knees bending in toward each other slightly and the right foot back of the line of flight. Almost all of his weight is on his left foot. His feet are slightly closer together than in the normal stance, in which the feet are apart a trifle less than the width of the shoulders. He takes the club straight back, keeping the face at that right angle. Then, with the hands and arms doing all the work, he strokes it squarely, the putter remaining at a perfect right angle to the ball right through the follow-up.

Nerves play an important part in the putting picture. They have beaten and bothered the greatest of putters, Hogan included. I'm no psychiatrist, so I'm not going to prescribe for your nerves. But it's only common sense that a natural confidence in your putting game will take you a long way toward success on the green. That confidence will come only by continuous practice at both stroking the ball itself and reading the green. Neither Ben nor I nor anyone else need tell you the value of putting. A good putter can be one or sometimes two strokes off the pace on the fairways and then make it up and even go ahead on the green. Hogan's forte is that short 8-feet-and-under putt. I would hate to have to count the strokes he has gained on yours truly in tournament play with his accurate putter.

As a little example of this deadly accuracy, let me refer once again to the Open at Oakmont in 1953. On the thirteenth green, Ben found his ball 30 feet away from the hole. There was what I call a "hog's back," a fancy name for a big bump, between the ball and the hole. Ben had the grass and the bump lined up correctly, and he hit the ball hard. If the ball hadn't gone in, it would have run right off the green. He canned it, of course. Ben takes a chance like this only when he's pretty sure the odds are in favor of his holing the putt.

At the Masters Tournament in 1952, it was the same story. He had a sidehill lie 8 feet out on the sixteenth hole at Augusta. This particular green slopes down toward the tee and the hole is a tricky one. Hogan's ball was on the left-hand side, below the cup, and in bumpy territory. He canned the putt by sending it uphill and looking for that break which would curve it right for the cup. He got it.

Don't look for your putter to produce such miracles as these. Be satisfied with those steady two-a-green putts and you'll be doing fine.

SCORING-AREA SHOTS

What we call the "scoring area"—from 125 to 130 yards off the green—is an aspect of the game which I often think was put into golf especially for Ben. It's an accepted fact that when he is hitting from this area, his next shot is very likely to be a 6- or 8-foot putt. Ben's accuracy from this part of the fairway close to the green is legendary.

A lot of his ability in this department comes from that wedge play of his. The heavy sand wedge, usually used for trap shots, is his best friend when he's in close. He hits the shot with a low trajectory and puts plenty of backspin on his ball. The backspin tends to make the shot drop dead at a point only a short distance from where it originally hit the green. Ben never tries for distance with this shot, nor does he strain to give the shot loft. *He trusts the loft of the club itself*. He hits it from the semiprofile stance. The left foot is out a bit and his feet are not opened wide. The knees are slightly bent and the grip is applied 2 inches from the end of the shaft. On this type of shot, he never tries to kill the ball. He wants a backspin which the ball will lose if it travels more than 150 yards in the air.

This wedge club is put to good use by Ben on those rare occasions when he gets himself stuck in a trap. But the manner in which he extricates himself is astonishing. The Hogan philosophy in a trap is to hole out in two strokes. I don't think he'd advise that philosophy for the average player, however. The latter must have only one objective: get out of the trap. If his ball stops rolling near the cup and he can sink his first putt, so much the better. But only the Ben Hogans can shoot for the cup from a trap. For this shot, again, the course charting must be taken into consideration. Sand has different textures. A fine sand makes it impossible to apply backspin to the ball. Thus you must allow for more roll. When Ben blasts out, the leading edge of his wedge does not hit the sand until the trailing edge does. Rather than bring his swing to an abrupt halt once contact has been made, he follows straight through on it. He takes a firm footing in the sand—but his mind is on that green.

A lot of people ask about the amount of sand that should be taken when in a trap. There is only one answer—"It all depends." It depends on the lie and the texture of the sand. If the ball is in fine, powdery sand, it's a good idea to take less. If it is buried in heavier sand, then to get out of the trap you must take plenty of sand with you. The amount of distance you are looking for on a particular trap shot is another factor which figures importantly in the excavation job. Hogan always expects not only to get on the green from a trap, but to get as close to the cup as possible. With this thought in mind, he hits the ball *before* taking any sand. A sand-digging shot may not give him the distance he wants.

The rest of Hogan's game is something which took him about thirty years to develop. He wouldn't be able to teach you many of the details in only a few lessons. From putter to driver, he would offer assorted tips which he has put to good use over the years. I must add a note of warning here. Special tips from Hogan or any other professional not acquainted with your style may or may not help your particular game. Ben could tell you how he does it, but some of his moves on a course might be the worst thing in the world for you to try. The only person actually qualified to equip your game with the appropriate tricks is your own pro. It's his job to know your needs. A conscientious home pro should be eager to build up the game of each player at his club. It's a matter of sheer pride with him, and common business sense as well.

Hogan's driving game is a perfect example of controlled power. Although some can outdrive him off the tee, Ben is a consistent 260- to 270-yard driver, which is a lot of distance for a man of his size. That delayed power is the generator of his distance. He plays this shot off his left side, of course. His stance is slightly closed and his toes are pointing out a bit, to give him better balance. He digs that right foot in, and uses a swing which is power-jammed at the base.

Hogan's precision with irons has not been matched by anybody in my golfing memory except Byron Nelson, and Lord Byron is considered by some to be the greatest iron player the game has ever seen. Hogan's steady skill in this department stems, in a large part, from his ability to control his every move, which in turn controls the ball. Ben would consider *hitting down on an iron shot* an important item during this lesson of yours. A player of his type and caliber almost always hits down on a ball in order to achieve underspin which keeps the ball in control. Ben would point out that the common fault among average swingers is the tendency to take turf behind the ball, instead of in front of it, as he does. Usually the novice takes turf behind the ball because he has started his address with most of his weight

Take turf in front of your ball

on the right foot and then fails to bring that weight over to the left on the downswing. Ben shifts his weight—and does it rapidly—at the top of his swing. This automatically forces his swing to dip lowest in front of the ball. Shift your weight to the left foot, take turf in front of the ball, and the chances are good that you'll be hitting down on it as he does.

Ben has a pet theory on this spinning business. I've spoken of overspin and underspin earlier in this chapter, but these are actually just expressions of mine. Hogan contends there's no such thing as overspin. "The only time there is overspin

192

on a shot is when it's topped," he says. "You've got to have underspin on a ball in order to get it up in the air. This overspin term is incorrect. What is actually meant is *a small amount of underspin*. When you see a ball hit the green and take off instead of dropping dead, people say it has overspin. I don't think so. The player simply put too little underspin on the ball."

A good deal of Ben's control secret lies in this factor, in my opinion. He uses a maximum of underspin. It's a rare day that you see iron shots hit by Ben Hogan running wild. He's a golfing scientist who has made a life study of the game, and he works on a formula until he's got it down pat. On an iron shot his blade contacts the ball first, in a downward motion, and then takes turf afterward as the blow continues downward. He hits the ball sharply, but without straining to raise it. Rather he lets the loft of the club take care of getting the ball off the ground.

That's an important concept for your thinking department. Trust that club of yours. The best technicians in the world have shaped and slanted it to make the specific shot at hand. You don't have to compensate for any deficiency in the club. That deficiency lies in the golfer.

Ben is particularly deadly with the five iron, a club which gives more underspin to a ball than any other stick in the bag. The five iron is the dividing club between long and short irons and is absolutely invaluable to the golfer who really knows how to use it.

If you came away from a lesson with Ben retaining even half of these tips, that Sunday afternoon foursome of yours would see a lot better game of golf. But one thing should remain uppermost in the minds of those seeking help with their golf game. You've got to put in those hours of practice in order to be a better golfer. Your home pro can give you plenty of help, a good deal more than any correspondence course or book on the subject. But in the final analysis, it's up to you. And Ben knows this better than anyone else in golf, having spent more hours on the practice tee than Snead, Nelson, and myself combined. The final result—the "click" of a solid wood shot soaring far down the fairway—is well worth the hours and days of effort.

CHAPTER 9

HOGAN AT CARNOUSTIE

Through the years, the British Open has become golf's ivy-covered tower. But tradition, an important item to the British, would not have been upheld had Ben Hogan refused to risk his reputation on the Carnoustie course in 1953, under strange conditions. The great players in history have won it—Ted Ray, Harry Vardon, Bobby Jones, Gene Sarazen, Walter Hagen, Bobby Locke. The British refuse to recognize the true worth of even the most famous golfer until he has captured their Open. For over a hundred years, it has been played on such ancient courses as Ganton, St. Andrews, and Carnoustie. The British and the Scots wanted to see Hogan in person. The stories about him that had crossed the ocean were too extraordinary to be true. But at Carnoustie on July 6–10 of 1953, the little man from Texas showed tradition-minded England and Scotland that they need not be wary of classing him with their all-time golf heroes.

Many consider Carnoustie the birthplace of golf. I haven't seen the course myself but I have played on other British layouts, and many people, Ben included, have described Carnoustie to me. As his scores made perfectly obvious, Hogan wasn't too impressed by the course. According to the British Press, which dogged Ben's footsteps and recorded his remarks, Hogan found Carnoustie's fairways much wider than those of championship courses in this country, the green approaches much less lightly trapped, and the greens themselves only slightly contoured. He allowed that it was a long course. They used tiger tees (tees moved back from their normal position) which stretched Carnoustie to 7,400 yards. But length was its only difficult feature.

I have learned to expect such statements from Ben. Had he lost the tournament, these remarks would have come back to haunt him. I can just see it in the London sports pages— "The Great American Golfer, who said Carnoustie wasn't difficult enough for him, finished a poor twelfth this afternoon in the British Open, behind six Englishmen, three Frenchmen, one South African, and the Champion of Afghanistan. . . ." But Ben is no diplomat; he doesn't consider all the possible ramifications of such remarks. He was asked what he thought of the course and he simply answered the question.

As a matter of fact, when I played in England on the Ryder Cup team in 1949, my reaction to English courses was quite similar to Ben's. Somehow, when you are fully aware of the part England and Scotland have played in golf history, you expect to get a special thrill trudging through the hallowed sand traps and strolling down the fairways on the courses where they invented the game. The Ryder Cup matches were played at Ganton, outside of London, and I can best describe the course as a sort of Pennsylvania Turnpike with tees. You could have called me Hooker Demaret during those 1949 matches but I always managed to stay on the fairway anyway, by hook or crook. (That's a joke, son.) The British golf architects allow history to overawe them, in my opinion. Instead of placing bunkers where a bad shot is penalized, as they do in this country, the British let the obstacles remain exactly where the gophers made them centuries ago. You can push a drive straight down the middle 280 yards, and land in a big trap right in the center of the fairway. They answer your complaints in tones of disbelief. "Fill it up and then build another some place else? Why, that hole was dug in the time of William the Conqueror!"

I'm told that at first glance, Carnoustie seems to be all one color, a green blended with brown. "A lot of times you couldn't tell whether your ball was on the fairway or in the rough," Ben said. When the English build a course, they simply flatten out the tee and green and then mow a path between them. On at least six spots at Carnoustie a trap was placed in the middle of this mowed path, right at the perfect driving distance.

On American courses, the greenskeeper's job is an important one. He manicures his greens almost daily and cuts the fairway grass weekly. His is a seven-day-a-week job, fifty-two weeks a year. Carnoustie, on the other hand, feels a lawn mower on its fairways once a month and the greens get clipped on a weekly basis. The fairways themselves are unreliable, bumpy affairs which can do crazy things to a ball. You rarely get an even bounce and it is exceedingly difficult to make a shot drop dead.

Hogan calls Carnoustie "burn-happy." That's because there are two burns, or streams, which constantly crisscross the course. On one hole—the sixteenth—the larger Bary Burn crosses the fairway three times. Because of the heavy rainfall on the course—it's near the North Sea—drainage ditches abound. The ditches are 3 feet deep and cost a one-stroke penalty if you get in them. The one-stroke penalty doesn't bother a man as much as the possibility of breaking a leg in one of the ditches.

As for the rough, Hogan can't tell us too much about that because, as his scores show, he didn't spend much time there. But heather grows in the rough in clumps about a foot high and as wide as it can get. Another wild plant called gorse, a tall, thorny bush 4 and 5 feet high, is equally plentiful. If you hit into heather, it would take a piston-run steam driver to get you out. The less said about the gorse, the better. You simply take a stroke.

The area surrounding the course provides plenty of distractions. Carnoustie's practice tee is only a few hundred yards away from a British Army rifle range, and a man trying to concentrate there often must contend with a machine gun slamming in his ear. A railroad track runs alongside the first hole of the course. As Ben was about to tee up for his initial competitive round, a golf-minded engineer gave his whistle cord three good yanks in a "hello" to the American golfing champion. Then he stopped his train and waved.

At starting time, Ben stepped onto the course to find a woman sitting inside a little house off to one side and no other officials around at all, only a couple of contestants and the usual crowd of spectators. He almost teed off without get-

198

ting the okay—from whom or where, he didn't know—but shaking heads in the crowd told him no. Finally, the lone woman gave a little hand horn two beeps and the crowd smiled, indicating that it was time to tee off. It was an inauspicious start for what turned out to be one of the greatest golfing victories of our time. It seemed strange to Ben— he told me that he nearly broke out laughing when the horn beeped—after the auspicious and glamorous ways we run our tournaments over here. For anybody else but Hogan, the lack of fanfare might have had a deadening effect on the zeal with which he went after the British crown.

But Hogan knew what it was all about.

Everything which goes to make up the golfer we know as Ben Hogan was sharply illustrated last July on this feared Scottish seaside links known as Carnoustie. Hogan wrote golf history and carved for himself a special niche in sports with his convincing victory. It was the first time an American had won the British Open on his initial try, and it was the first time that proud Carnoustie had been played in under 70 strokes. Ben shot a 69 in his opening practice round and won the event with a record 68 on his last round.

The British had been literally begging Ben to come over and take a crack at their biggest event. British golfers, writers, and the public wanted him to test Carnoustie, and vice versa. And the American golf world wanted to see him go, too. Since I was perhaps partially responsible for turning this little guy loose on the Scots and their hallowed course, I was particularly interested in what he'd do over there. Don't get me wrong. It never entered my mind that Ben might lose.

Barring some extraordinary bad luck, I was confident that The Hawk could and would win it. I was just worried that my man Hogan would shoot such low scores with that small British ball that everybody over there would give up the game in despair. I didn't want to see all those nice British pros out of work.

But there were many who just couldn't believe that Hogan could make the long trip to Carnoustie and then beat an array of the world's best golfers on a strange course. Some thought the weather would bother Ben. "The wind and the squalls will hamper his game a good deal," they wrote. The weather changes violently during the day at many English and Scottish courses. (I guess that's why their golfers always walk as if they were bucking the wind.) A fellow can go out in the morning and play in bright sunshine, find himself drenched by sudden squalls at noon, and then get himself dried out by the sun by mid-afternoon. This weather factor, some thought, could account for as much as a seven-stroke difference. Carnoustie is particularly tough in this respect because its proximity to the North Sea guarantees a fair amount of moisture in the air as well as a stiff breeze.

However, the people who were counting on the elements to throw a monkey wrench into the delicate machinery of Ben's game weren't taking into consideration the wide variety of weather in America. It's true that the weather in Scotland bothered Ben, but such distractions were nothing new. The stiff Texas winds had bothered him before, yet he finished the Colonial Invitation in 1952 at Fort Worth with a 67, and the wind was blowing at 40 miles an hour. Sudden showers and quick weather changes are plentiful at such courses as Pebble Beach and the Riviera in California. Ben has both the ability and intelligence to adjust his game to bad weather.

Rain or shine, I knew Ben wasn't crossing the ocean to lose. Nor was he going for the money. The winner's end for the event is only $650. To a man who is having difficulty filling all the requests for one-day exhibition dates in the United States at $1,500 and $2,000 a crack, that isn't much of an inducement. Hogan went after the British Open simply to win it. In a sense, it was the final challenge.

For golfers in Britain, Ben had become a legendary figure, but one they never had seen in action. He had accompanied the Ryder Cup team as its nonplaying captain in 1949, but he had never hit a golf ball on a British course. The Scots in particular, having a special claim on golf, were anxious to have a look at his game.

Edinburgh's *Golf Monthly* ran an editorial under the headline, "Hogan, the Master—Come Over"—which, I think, sums up how the British Isles felt about Hogan. "Carnoustie, did he come and triumph, would impress the seal of Hogan's fame. In phantasy we see Hogan, the enigma, silent, austere, resolute, battling out of the wind-swept links of the Angus seaboard, one of the massive tests of the game in the world. Do not leave it too late, Ben, to take your place amongst the immortals and the supreme honour in the game. Scottish golfers, and especially Carnoustie, whose sons did so much for golf in your homeland, will take you to their hearts."

When Ben decided to make the trip, it not only delighted the Scots but eliminated any chance that they might one day say of the American champion, "Well, he never won the Open *over here!*" Actually ever since he had won his first U.S. Open with that 276 in 1948, Bantam Ben was in great demand over there. At first, when approached about it, he'd say bluntly, "What would it prove?" Then, after the auto mishap, he begged off, quite honestly, because he said "the cold weather bothers me since my accident."

The British Open ran from July sixth until the tenth, and during that time—and the ten days before when he practiced—the British and Scots saw enough of Ben Hogan to convince them that even Texans were not exaggerating his ability. They expected an austere, quiet little man and they got just that—he remained poker-faced right down to his last ace. From newspapermen, who knew his insistence on the bald truth, right down to the restaurant people, who had heard of his pickiness about food, the Scots got the real Hogan at Carnoustie.

He and Valerie arrived via plane ten days before the tournament was to start and were ticketed for the Bruce Hotel, which is right next to the course. The Bruce is a fine place, but it had no private baths, and Ben had it fixed in his mind that he was going to submerge his frame in hot water every night no matter what. So he took up an offer from Chick Allen, a National Cash Register executive who made the trip to see the Open, to stay at a private cottage the firm maintains 15 miles away from the course.

His very first day at Carnoustie, Ben went out for a practice round. In keeping with his approach to big tournaments, he did his best to be alone. He also insisted on paying the fourpence green fees. But they couldn't keep the people away. The Scots came out by the hundreds, just to watch him practice. Because he made no secret of his desire to practice alone, the newspapers printed headlines saying, "Lone Bird Hogan Stalks Carnoustie in Silence." If they were hoping that Ben would sit beneath a tree with them, balancing a cup of tea and gossiping about golf, they certainly had the wrong man. But they had the right golfer. Ben shocked British golf enthusiasts right down to their boots with his score. He shot a 69 on his first try at the course. That was one stroke lower than anyone else had ever shot in the 400 years Carnoustie had been in existence.

Arthur Lacey, who captained the British Ryder Cup team in 1951, watched the man getting in shape and he came away a confirmed Hogan admirer. "He scored more bull's-eyes than a military marksman on a nearby rifle range," the English pro said.

Like the weather, the smaller British ball was expected to give Hogan some trouble. The English use a ball 1.62 inches in diameter as compared to the 1.68-inch pellet we use in America. Ben, before he left, didn't think it would bother him, and when he got over there he found it actually helped. "He took to the British ball like a duck to water," Lacey said. "He found that it actually goes much farther than the American model. He liked the way it hugged the greens for putting, but it still did give him one problem. Ben found he could hit the ball so far that he had difficulty in judging the range for choice between his two and three irons." Now, that is the kind of problem I would like to face someday— too much distance.

In one session, Ben hit dozens of balls from the practice tee that lanky Cecil Timms, his thirty-three-year-old professional caddy, didn't have to move more than a few steps to retrieve. Everything was hit right at his feet.

Even after his startling 69-stroke practice round, one question remained as to his readiness. That was the little man's health. The strange weather and diet figured to have their effect on him. "I lost weight, came down with one of those really bothersome colds—my temperature hit one hundred on the last day—and I finished up a tired guy," Ben told me when he got back from England. When he walked into Shor's to attend the luncheon given in his honor the day he returned, Ben looked gaunt from that lost weight. He shuffled in almost as if he didn't have the strength to lift his feet. On three separate occasions during the British Open, he was given treatment for his back. "I'm very worried about Ben's health. He gets so tired," Valerie told a newsman in one of her rare interviews during the tournament. She had reason to worry. His blood pressure dropped to ninety before the last round started.

However, Hogan kept it to himself. He didn't want anybody to know of his illness. If he was going to lose, there would be no convenient alibis to fall back on.

The tournament itself consisted of two qualifying rounds of eighteen holes each and then a seventy-two-hole grind for the championship. The qualifying rounds are intended to weed out the field, narrow it down to the golfers who matter. Plenty of duffers get into an event such as the British Open—an Open is just what the word means, as opposed to an Invitational—and some sort of qualifying test must be rigged to make the field manageable.

The qualifying rounds were held on Monday and Tuesday over the Burnside course, another eighteen-hole layout which runs alongside of Carnoustie and at several spots along the way mixes in with the main course itself. It's a confusing layout to follow and Ben claimed that he needed a guide to help him find his way around. He had a crowd of 8,000 with him when he teed off for the first qualifying round that Monday afternoon. Golf lovers from all over the globe found themselves being elbowed into the creeks dotting the course as the mob rushed to have a look at the American golfer in action.

Our Texas Irishman wasn't looking for any records this first time out. Although he just wanted to qualify, he still finished the first nine two under par. Coming back in, he had a 38 to give him a 70 for the day and the British onlookers seemed surprised. "He actually smiled a little," somebody said. Hogan gave the crowd an indication of things to come on the seventh hole, which is 363 yards long, when he hit a 260-yard drive right down the fairway and then dropped his approach only 5 feet away from the pin. He canned the putt for a birdie three.

It was a different story on Tuesday. In this second qualifying round, he shot a 75 to finish in an eight-way tie for fourteenth place and the skeptics had a field day. Ben had a tough time with his putter on the greens and ran into some typical Carnoustie weather—it rained five times between morning and afternoon, twice hard. "They were chewing-gum greens if I ever saw them," Ben said, but if the people were looking for an alibi, they came away disappointed. "All in all, I didn't play well today," was all he would say.

Plenty of people agreed with him. A London newspaperman, watching him, arched his eyebrows and asked, "Who are we watching? This man doesn't play like Hogan. Rather like his grandmother, I'd say." On the ninth hole of that second qualifying round, two U.S. Marine Corps lieutenants were properly horrified to see the way Ben was touring the course. "The government shouldn't have allowed him to come over here and play so badly," one of them was overheard to say. Maybe the lieutenant thought it was bad for international relations, or something.

When the tournament started, the onlookers got another surprise. Instead of making a lavish affair of his lunch—and giving everyone in Scotland a chance to bother him out of his skin with a million questions—Ben ate a quiet box lunch, sent to the course by Valerie, with Cecil Timms, his caddy. This became his daily routine.

Bobby Locke, the South African, had set the qualifying pace with a 136, and Frank Stranahan, the Toledo millionaire amateur, had led the U.S. delegation, which included Lloyd Mangrum, with a two-day total of 144. Roberto di Vicenzo shot excellent golf in the qualifying rounds and continued to play steady golf throughout the tournament.

Stranahan led the field after Wednesday's official opening round of eighteen holes with a two-under-par 70. Di Vicenzo shot a 72. Ben had a 73 and he was thoroughly annoyed at himself afterward. "I don't mind scoring high, but I hate stupid mistakes," he snapped. Ben kept pace with par—36—on the way out, even though he missed a 9-foot putt on the ninth green by inches. He started out the back nine by playing one-under-par golf for the first six holes. But he proceeded to bogey the next two holes, missing putts of 9 and 3 feet. The weather again bothered him, a hailstorm holding him up for fifteen minutes on the fifth green.

After this poor first round, Ben gave a fine illustration of his cool, concise powers of analysis to John Derr. He calmly explained to the Columbia Broadcasting System sports director just what he had done wrong. "I made three bad mistakes on the last three holes," he said. On the sixteenth, he played that left-to-right fade, only to fade the ball too much and let the wind carry it into the face of a deep bunker. He got out of that trouble, but then missed his putt on the sixteenth green. On the seventeenth, Ben explained that he'd hit his two-iron second shot "fat," failing to get all the ball on the face of the club. It dropped too quickly and didn't reach the green. He pulled out of that predicament by slamming an iron shot low and straight to the pin, against the wind, only to have his putt die right at the edge of the cup. On the eighteenth, Ben told Derr that he made a mistake in his drive. "I cut the tee shot too much," he said. It went to the right and wound up in a bunker. Ben had to play his next shot safe to ensure against putting his ball in a creek. His seven iron, again, went straight for the flag, so straight, in fact, that it hit the pin and bounced 6 feet away. His putt, once more, ran right to the cup, looked down into its depths, and decided to hang on the lip.

His bad back and cold kicked up on him on Wednesday evening and Ben appeared on the tee for Thursday's second round after a sleepless night. Nevertheless he started well, and a wave of excitement ran through the crowd as they watched Hogan birdie six of the first eight holes. But it soon became apparent that Ben's putter was still misbehaving. Despite that fast start, he was not to deliver any earth-shaking score on this second round.

He had what he called a "dumb shot" on the seventh hole when he put a four wood into the trap at the right of the green. On the ninth hole, he chipped weakly. Even his putting was bothering him on the first nine; he missed a putt (and a birdie three) by the width of the ball on the first hole.

On the last six holes, however, he played consistently excellent golf and began to close in on the leaders. His tee-to-green play was perfect and his putting game began to behave. He finished the day with a respectable 71. That left him only two strokes behind Britain's Dai Reese and Scotland's Eric Brown, who were tied for the lead with 142. Stranahan had fallen off the pace with a 74.

After Ben's Thursday round, an old Scot came by at the clubhouse and remarked to Hogan, "Aye, it looks like being a tie." Apparently he had been looking at the club scoreboard which showed ten players, including Reese, Hogan, and Brown, within four strokes of each other. Ben, characteristically, waited for the Scot to leave, then said quietly, "There isn't going to be any tie."

The last day of the tournament, in which two complete rounds were played, was a cloudy and shower-filled day. Ben Hogan, under a plaid cap and wrapped in two sweaters, walked up to start the first of those 36 holes at 10:27 A.M.

Below is a table of Carnoustie's par and Hogan's two final rounds. Figures can be deceiving, I'm told, but these are crystal-clear. They show two rounds of steady brilliant golf under enormous pressure.

CARNOUSTIE PAR:

Out	4	4	4	4	4	5	4	3	4	...36
In	4	4	3	5	4	3	4	5	...36
										72

HOGAN FIRST ROUND (last day):

Out	4	3	4	5	5	4	3	3	4	...35
In	3	4	5	2	4	4	3	6	4	...35
										70

HOGAN FINAL ROUND:

Out	4	4	4	4	3	4	4	3	4	...34
In	4	4	4	2	5	4	3	4	4	...34
										68

Ben's iron shots were unbelievably accurate in the morning, but he still had some trouble with his putting. However, every time he ran across a bad hole he refused to let his nerves shake him loose. He'd fight back with a birdie. He was one under after three holes, but then took successive bogeys, because of poor putting, on the fourth and fifth. It looked like the perfect place for him to fold. The British Open championship seemed to hang in the balance. But he fought back with birdies on the fifth and sixth and then had four more on the back nine to offset two more putt-produced bogeys. His double bogey on the seventeenth was a six, two over par, and destroyed what could have been a superb 68 round. He drove into a bunker on the hole and then took three putts on the green. Such a hole, at the start of the back stretch, so to speak, might well have proved a morale crusher for a lesser man. But Ben bounced right back with a birdie four on the eighteenth. Then he sat down with his caddie and ate the box lunch Valerie had sent over and puffed away on his cigarettes. "I smoked forty cigarettes on these two rounds," the nervous Cecil Timms said, "and I know Hogan smoked more. Between us we must have gone through a hundred of the things."

As Hogan was polishing off the last of his box lunch, Bob Brumby, the American golf writer, came over and asked, "Ben, is there anything I can do for you?" Hogan just smiled and said, "Yeah. You can sink a few putts for me, Bob." Then he turned quietly to his caddie and said, "Let's go out there and win it."

When the morning scores reached me in New York, I realized that he was tied with Di Vicenzo for the lead. The Argentinian had put two 72s back to back in the second and third rounds. I wondered just how low a score Hogan was going to post for that final eighteen. I knew he was winding up for that one big round which he always holds in reserve for just the right spot. That moment had arrived. I didn't rate Di Vicenzo, Stranahan, or Carnoustie a lick of a chance against him. Later in the day, I picked up the phone and put in a call to Harry Grayson, the Newspaper Enterprise Association sports editor, and asked him what had happened.

"What do *you* think he did?" Harry countered.

"Well, I figure he must have shot something low in the sixties."

"You're not too far off," Harry answered. "The guy shot a sixty-eight to win. That's all."

My partner Ben played masterful golf on that last eighteen. He never took more than two putts on any green and on the fifth hole he dispensed with putting entirely. His second shot to a sloping green rolled back to a bunker and it looked like a difficult chip shot. Ben looked the situation over carefully, studied it, took his time. Then he thrilled the huge gallery with an unbelievable 50-foot chip right into the hole.

On the first nine, he kept knocking down par after par. On the back nine he was short with his second shot twice—on the twelfth and the fourteenth—and he had putting trouble as well. But he made up for these lapses on the thirteenth with a difficult birdie two, and on the sixteenth where he was four under fours.

It was on the fifteenth hole, after his drive, that Hogan realized, for the first time, that he would probably win. He started the hole tied for the lead. Three were in ahead of him with 286—Dai Reese, Stranahan, and Peter Thompson. Antonio Cerda, who was playing behind him on the thirteenth, had one over the level fours which Carnoustie uses in place of our par. As Hogan strode down the fairway, he veered toward John Derr who was, as usual, broadcasting from the middle of the fairway. Derr gave Hogan the news of who was in with what scores. Then he mentioned Cerda and his score at that moment.

"Is he on the tee or green?" Ben asked.

"He's on the tee," Derr answered.

Ben looked straight ahead and puffed solemnly on his

cigarette. He stood still in the middle of the fairway for a moment. Cerda was not going to make it. That seemed sure. Hogan's playing partner for that round, Hector Thompson, watched from a few yards away. Then Ben looked at Derr and said, "Thanks, John. That'll be all." The British Open was over.

"I rate that one sentence my all-time sports thrill," Derr told me in New York. "When he said, 'That'll be all,' I knew Ben wasn't going to lose."

In recalling those last three holes, Hogan puts it this way. "I thought I'd win, as long as I didn't do anything foolish." Playing steady golf, he got his par on the fifteenth, then on the sixteenth and again on the seventeenth. Now he turned for home. With hundreds of Scots crowding every inch of space along the final fairway and green, Ben mechanically worked his way to the championship with a birdie four.

A press conference and two radio broadcasts followed immediately and Ben did not have time even to change his shoes or get a jacket. At the presentation ceremony, the jacket helped produce the kind of misunderstanding which has dogged Ben all his golfing life. The tournament's leading players and members of the championship committee, along with the crowd, were forced to wait fifteen minutes in the rain while Ben stood in the doorway of the committee room shivering in his playing sweaters. He refused to receive the British trophy without a coat.

The Carnoustie crowd took few pains to hide its irritation. "Why are we waiting?" people muttered. Roberto di Vicenzo, the Argentine star, gave his watch a look and then left. But Ben wasn't budging. He felt that it would have been an affront to the British to receive their most prized golf trophy dressed only in his playing sweaters. Besides, he was a dangerously tired guy. He said as much himself. "I am only forty [now Ben!] but I feel like sixty." The rain beating down could have seriously affected a man in his condition.

Anyway, the Hawk stayed in the shelter of the doorway waiting for his jacket. When finally he arrived at the presentation dais, Ben was greeted with a noticeable lack of warmth and enthusiasm by the crowd. He won't talk about it now. It's an incident long forgotten.

There were 15,000 people waiting to hear Ben's remarks and see him accept the trophy from Henry Turcan, the committee chairman. A smart master of the art of flattery or a wise public relations man would have seized this opportunity to butter up the boys for future favors and a good press. Ben could have gushed all sorts of flattering remarks and the people would have loved it. Instead, he refused to say that he would return for the next year's British Open and added that he was not going to play any tournament golf until March. No matter what other remarks, or perhaps even little white lies about his certain return next year, would have pleased his listeners, Ben just had to stick to the bold truth. Tactless, yes. But a refreshing note in a sports world too often dominated by press agents.

As for his wife, Valerie, very few even saw her at Carnoustie. As the mob gathered to watch Ben's putter bring him victory on the final green, she tried to edge her way forward—and then apologized when she'd accidentally nudged somebody. "How is it going?" she asked a British reporter. He recognized her and soon the policemen who had been brushing her back were rushing her forward. But she stayed in the background, outside the players' enclosure.

"I'll wait out here," she said to reporters. "It was Ben's victory. I'll just stay here and wait for him."

As the crowd finally broke up after the presentation and Valerie reached her husband's side, Hector Thomson, who shot the lowest score of any Scot in the event, was talking to the British press. Hector had played with Ben on the last eighteen holes and the newsmen were interested in the fact that Ben seemed indifferent to the reactions of the gallery. He didn't show any emotion about it, one of the paper boys said.

"Not a bit of it," Hector answered. "Every time they applauded a shot, he'd murmur, 'Thank you.' You had to be close to hear it—but it always was there." And then Hector had the last word. "He's a fine sportsman as well as a great golfer."

Jimmy Demaret has been prominent in golfing circles for more than two decades. He hails originally from Texas and today makes his home in Houston, although he spends a good part of each year at the Concord Hotel at Lake Kiamesha, New York, where he is the head golf professional. Demaret is the only golfer to have won the important Masters Tournament in Augusta three times, and during the year 1947 he was the top money winner among professional golfers. He began his long career in golf as a caddy in Texas—as did his best friend in the game, Ben Hogan—and over a twenty-five-year period stroked his way to the top of the golf world, winning just about every tournament in the country as well as his share of Ryder Cup matches. Today Demaret describes himself as a "semi-tour" golfer, meaning that he plays in a few of the tournaments on the golf circuit but not in all of them. He also acts in an advisory capacity for the MacGregor Sporting Goods Company, helping to design clubs and other articles of equipment, and for the Palm Beach Company. This book is his first venture into the writing field.